RISE and SHINE!

How to Live a Life of Resilience

and Perform at Your Potential

MICHELLE PERDUE, M.Ed.

DEDICATION

To my husband and children, simply put, I love you. You are the wind beneath my wings, and the calm during my storms of life. You have shown me the true meaning of unconditional love and for that I am beyond grateful. Your daily hugs, kisses, and loving words give me the momentum I need to rise and shine and embrace who I am, and, most importantly, who I am becoming.

To my mother, your warm spirit and unending support encouraging me to follow my dreams is priceless. The laughs we've had, the stories we've shared, and the dreams that were born, will live in my heart forever. You are dearly loved and appreciated.

To my father, you left us way too soon. When you left so did my child-hood hero and some wonderful memories that we shared. I learned from you. I grew from you and it's because of your guidance, I was inspired to come to peace with you. Rest easy and love always.

To my brothers and sister, you are my sunshine. I am so lucky to have each of you in my life. The memories we've shared will forever unite us as we vow to never let anything divide us. I love you to the moon and back. Your big sis forever and always.

To my grandparents, you both were the best grandparents anyone could have hoped for. You were my rock and shield from the time I was born until the day you died. The morals and values you've instilled in me are reflective of the work I do and how I choose to live my life. You may be gone, but you will never be forgotten- love always.

To Linda Pelham, thank you for being there for me when I needed it the most. Your kindness, support and loving heart will forever be remembered. It's friends like you who make the world a brighter place—love always.

CONTENTS

FOREWORD

The road to live a life of resilience is bumpy with many twists and turns. Around every corner the proverbial "punch in the gut" waits to lay you out flat. In order to Rise and Shine each day, putting your best foot forward and performing at your best consistently takes resilience.

A life of purpose and meaning is a contact sport and resilience is a critical tool that you need to nurture and to carry with you to perform at your potential. Resilience is about belief in oneself and contributing to something larger than you. In *Rise and Shine*, Michelle Perdue shares best performance strategies to nurture and to develop your potential for resilience.

We all have some level of capacity to pick ourselves up when we are down—to get back in the game after setbacks—and Michelle Perdue's real-life experiences show how each of us can develop a resilient mindset and be better prepared for that next twist and turn.

As we navigate a world beset by a public health crisis, social injustice, economic inequity, and social media influence threatening to compromise our values on almost every meaningful subject, our ability to have a clear purpose and resilience is critical for personal fulfillment and happiness. I am convinced that a positive attitude and an abundance of gratitude are critical to reach our potential.

Theatre and life are an ideal stage to examine resilience because of its balance of the physical, mental, and emotional. Every day, the next show and the bright lights will test those of us who are expected to perform with grace while under fire. We succeed and fail multiple times and these tussles with adversity help us to sharpen our resilience continually. It is not about avoiding adversity; it is developing the skills to accept the positive gifts adversity is meant to offer us and to keep us moving forward in order to perform at our potential.

Enjoy this compelling journey with Michelle as she has lived every minute of it. Her story to Rise and Shine, and how she developed and strengthened her own resilience took place through the course of her life and contributed to her success. This is a great read that you will enjoy. You will take away many practical tools so you can develop the resilience needed in order to perform to your potential daily.

It's time to Rise and Shine!

Pam Borton
ICF Master Executive Coach | Professional Speaker | Author
NCAA Final Four Coach | Winningest Coach in Basketball History
 at the University of Minnesota

PREFACE

My inspiration and motivation for writing this book runs overwhelmingly deep. A depth so ingrained in my being that I am no longer content harboring stories at the expense of my fears and ego. The trajectory of my life has brought me to a place where I want to share my stories and lessons learned to uplift humanity and cultivate resiliency. It's a place that invigorates my spirit and gives me a sense of inner peace. It's a peace that stems from wanting to be a light, but more importantly to illuminate the light of someone else—YOU!

Your struggles, fears and insecurities inspire me to do the work I do. I want to be the catalyst that ignites your soul and inspires change. I want to support you in your journey to seeing what's possible when you minimize your fears to maximize your potential. How do you do that? You do that by getting out of your way and taking responsibility for your life so you can rise and shine to become the best version of you. My gut tells me you want to be better and do better. It tells me you are no longer satisfied living a mediocre life and you want to see brighter days. If I am accurate in my assumptions, know that your heart's desires are possible.

My goal is that you will read each chapter with an open heart and allow my stories to inspire you to re-connect with your own. To be a voice to your stories so they liberate you rather than limit you by accepting your past to welcome a more gratifying future. My goal is that you will not only read the messages that are meant to equip you with the tools needed to boost your resilience, but also to apply them with intention to optimize your results. This is your time to live your best life; not tomorrow, next week or next year, but today. The world deserves the best of you and so do you. Now, let's rise and shine!

THE COURAGE TO RISE AND SHINE

Please don't shoot! This was the only thought running through my mind as my father stood at the entry of the doorway aiming a gun at the temple of his head. I wanted with every part of my being to escape the dread and doom that was about to take place. However, with his threatening and foreboding body blocking the front door and creating an unwavering barrier to my safety, I was beginning to lose hope. Consequently, I was mentally shackled to images that no child should ever have to witness.

The thought of seeing blood, a lifeless body, and the end of the wishful dream of coming to live with my father deadened my spirit. "If you tell, I'll kill myself." Paralyzed by fear, it appeared to me as if he would accomplish his intentions and I would succumb to his wishes. After all, I was only 11-years old and who was I to disobey my father? A man who found laughter in moments of uncertainty. A man who showed resilience after losing his mother at an early age.

A man who was admired by many as he sat on the deacon board at a well-known church in the community. "How can you be a man of God and appear as if you are doing everything good, yet you are capable of doing something undeniably bad?" I was confused.

The short-lived secret distorted my past and present thoughts of who my father really was. Was he the man I had always hoped for or was that just a figment of my imagination? This left me to question his character and the solace I found in his words during moments of unrest. However, I had no idea the ramifications this experience would have on my performance in life. I often wondered how I would show up in life and navigate my way against what felt like insurmountable odds. Needless to say, this experience, among others, would impact my life in a profound way.

You see, there have been times in my life when I have felt paralyzed. Interestingly, my lack of mobility did not stem from a physical impairment or disability, but rather life altering experiences that would eventually compromise my ability to perform at my potential. As a result, those moments of hopelessness and discontentment turned into days, weeks, and, regrettably, years.

The truth is, the defining moments of my life, including the aforementioned decades-old encounter with my father, were beginning to take a toll. I could envision my heart's desires and wildest dreams; however, I wasn't delivering the performance needed to bring them to fruition. It seemed as if I lacked the skills of resiliency to face and overcome some of the most profound adversities in my life. As a result, I wasn't driving my life in the direction I knew I needed to go to align with my ambitions. I wanted to rise and shine, yet I had begun to feel as if fear ruled my life as I sought my true identity. I knew I needed to step up and embrace the role I wholeheartedly knew I was born to fill, to empower others by helping them find their voice, embrace the power within, and ultimately change their lives in the most meaningful way. Unfortunately, my fears and the accumulation of past experiences overshadowed my ambitions.

I began to notice patterns in my life that enabled me to settle for mediocrity and I desperately wanted to escape. How could I be so sure? My heavy spirit would no longer allow me to sleep at night. There were many nights I lay restless, knowing that I was hindering my passion and purpose in life. I would see other people living fully and embracing their power in hopes that maybe one day that could be me. Over time, I repeatedly wrote down goals only to find myself writing them again and again. I began to lose hope. I began to question God's intention. "Why did you give me this vision of empowering others only to make me feel disempowered?" What sense does that make? Fortunately, as a way to cope with my ambivalent feelings, I relied on my acting skills and ability to write and perform poetry to channel my energy. It served as a coping mechanism to squash the pain. It provided me a creative outlet to channel my frustrations and conflicting thoughts in a productive and cathartic way, and for that, I am grateful.

As I list these mental and emotional barriers, I realize for some of you who know me, this information may come as a surprise. You may look at my life and see the things I have accomplished thus far and be unable to digest or understand my sentiments. I understand...I get it. However, I need you to understand this. When someone is not using their gifts and talents to the best of their ability and only lives a fraction of their life, they not only rob themselves, but also the people who they are meant to help. Bottom line: I want to live fully. I want my cup to overflow with self-love, inner peace and a purposeful life driven by passion and intentionality. I want to face my fears so that I can rise and shine to become my potential, and I want to share what I've learned with you.

I believe we are put on this earth to identify our purpose and then to use our gifts and talents to be of service to others. Then, as we allow ourselves to shine, we can provide light to help someone else shine even brighter. Can you imagine how different the world would be if we embraced our fears to become who we were meant to be? If we stopped placing blame and judgement on ourselves by stepping up and owning every part of our being? For those of you who feel inspired by these questions and want to perform at your potential, I encourage you to continue reading. I want to inspire you to leave the old you behind and develop the skill set to rise and shine. It is my hope that you will open a new chapter in your life. I sincerely mean this both literally and figuratively. This can be achieved by facing the unknown and leaning in to the momentum of life's gravitational forces. This will allow you to achieve massive results and take the center stage of life to deliver your most resilient and acclaimed performance. Give your life performance the attention it needs to thrive so that you can show up emotionally and mentally ready to take charge.

The way I see it, life is made up of a series of unscripted and unrehearsed performances. Every day you wake up you are given an opportunity to rise and shine as the best version of yourself and connect with others on a meaningful level through your gifts and talents. How sad would it be to have others invested in your "performance" only to not show up, but rather hide behind the curtains of life, leaving them wanting for more? Just think about it; every time you share your hopes and dreams with others and shortchange them by not delivering on your promise, you rob them of their investment. Their investment in you! I know this to be true because I've been there. Therefore, when life begins to take its toll and you are faced with obstacles such as those mentioned in this book, let my principles guide you and support you in your journey to consistently rise and deliver a captivating performance. This is what I want for you. Are you ready?

As the creator of your life, you are also the author of your life's story. If you are not satisfied with certain performances or outcomes, you have an opportunity to rise and learn from those experiences. Let the ending of that particular chapter in your life serve you well and propel you to greater heights, but even more so, let it move you into the next chapter of your life. Let it give you a new way of being and thinking so that you are more informed about how to lead your life with resiliency. Therefore, let each potentially defining moment in your life be the catalyst for change through self-reflection, gratitude, and intentional behavior. Those defining moments will inevitably consist of drama and conflict, but it wouldn't be a good story if they didn't.

It's the drama in our lives that brings us to a higher level of consciousness, forcing us as human beings to be more self-aware of what's happening outside ourselves. More importantly, we need to attend to what's happening within us. Needless to say, we should be editing our stories all the time to restore our resilience, deepen our understanding of who we are, and to bring to light the things that rob us of a story well told. It's our stories, which are manifested through our experiences that inform and shape our performance. No, we can't go back in time and change what has already happened, but we can change our response to the events in our lives, which will inevitably change the outcome. How powerful is that?

Will it be easy? No. Will it be worth it? Yes! Once you face the emotional and psychological barriers in your life head on, you will begin to see all that life has to offer and feel empowered with your ability to attain it. Doors will begin to open, your spirit will begin to rejoice, your actions will be in alignment with your hopes and dreams, your will to succeed will become infectious, and your life will begin to take on new meaning. Now, let's make it happen! If you have the desire to change and are willing to take the steps to get there, this is your time to rise and shine! The world is waiting to see your ultimate performance; they are waiting to see the bold, resilient you. They are waiting for your rise!

What's to Come in Each Chapter

In each chapter you will find the sustenance needed to feed your mind and soul so you can see what's possible. More importantly, you will find out how to take the steps necessary to achieve those things which seem impossible. Each chapter includes:

- personal stories to inspire you and elevate your performance in various stages of your life

- transformational words of wisdom to elevate your consciousness for risking bigger, thinking smarter, and living more boldly

- thought-provoking questions to allow for self-reflection and self-discovery

- quotes to entertain, inspire, and further your life toward achieving your potential

- poems to complement particular chapters to further deepen and enrich your reading experience

I Invite You to Continue Your Journey

During your journey of personal transformation, just like the storms of life, the experience can be unpredictable and overwhelming. It may test your fortitude and ability to survive whatever challenges you may be going through. There may be days when you feel as if you want to give up. When you would rather settle and take the easy road. For instance, you want to ask for a pay raise, but you don't. Instead, you settle for the amount that was given to you. You want to change careers, but you lack the confidence needed to transition from where you are to where you want to be. You want more out of life but can't find the time or resources to invest in your future.

During moments of self-doubt and inner turmoil, I want you to ask yourself, "If I am not willing to sacrifice for my goals, how can I expect to rise and become the person I need to be in order to accomplish my dreams?" It is those who are not willing to embrace the struggle, who focus on the results rather than the process who will, without question, undermine their potential and jeopardize their ambitions. Needless to say, resilience is reserved for the brave. Resilience is reserved for those who aren't afraid to step up and face the challenges life brings. They learn to take center stage of life and own it.

I know this journey will not always be easy. With all due respect, it's not supposed to be. Therefore, give life to your journey: embrace it, nurture it, and appreciate it. Just like you were created to bring life into the world, you are also equipped to step up and change it-one step, one moment, one performance at a time. Rise and shine...the world is waiting!

RISE AND SHINE
By: Michelle Perdue

I anxiously awaken to the beauty of the illuminous rising sun
Excited for the day, in all of its glory, yet it's barely begun
The thrill I seek lies in the quest of owning my greatness
For when I embrace the authentic me, I rise bold and audacious
Backbone erect, feet grounded to mother earth, as I stand in my truth
I rise and shine to stand in my purpose and do what I was born to do
I was born to conquer my debilitating and self-limiting fears,
Act beyond painful barriers causing blood, sweat, and tears
Give humanity a boost when darkness appears to have overshadowed their joy
Be the rainbow in the midst of their storms that aim to destroy
I am a believer and conceiver of my destiny as I create it day by day
That's why I rise and shine with confidence and sing His praise
When I rise, I give gratitude to those who have helped me to love myself

They've helped me to own my imperfections in spite of the cards I've been dealt
When I rise and shine, I feel as though I am in control and can achieve my best
I don't lose hope and get discouraged, I accept life happens, it's simply a test
My hope is you will rise and shine and see each day as a new beginning
Regardless of your past mistakes, flaws and failures, you're alive, you're winning
So when darkness falls and you lose your way and don't know which way to turn
Look back and reminisce about sunny days and all the life lessons learned
Let the sun illuminate your thoughts to bring your greatest ideas to fruition
You are not worthless news, act as if you are in vogue, the latest edition
It's time to rise and shine and let your beauty, passion, and gifts rise with the sun
Embrace who you are, there's no one like you, you're the only one
Let the light within you ignite your soul through the good and bad times
Accept you are destined for greatness; it's your time to rise and shine

Chapter 1

CONSIDER OTHERS IN YOUR PURSUIT OF HAPPINESS

*Being considerate of others will take your children
further in life than any college degree.
Marian Wright Edelman*

As a child, I had the luxury of living with my mother and grand-parents at different stages of my life. Each household had its own way of functioning and exposing me to the realities of the world. If I had to contrast the two, my mother's small two-bedroom subsidized housing in the projects seemed to be one-dimensional the majority of the time, meaning it was predictable in the sense of daily rituals and expectations. My grandparents', on the other hand, was more complex and multi-dimensional, leaving you to wonder what could happen at any given moment. The combination of an alco-holic husband and a few children who were likely to follow in the same footsteps presented its own unique challenges. Let's just say there were moments when I felt as if we were the epitome of a reality show. I suspect some of our neighbors would agree and so would some of the local police officers. However, there was one common-ality between both households: they both were a place called home.

Growing up with my mother and having little means was a way of life I had become accustomed to, and because of that, I was not fazed by our lack of material possessions. I learned to appreciate the things I did have, primarily because I didn't know any different. At one point, while living with my mother, I assumed brown beans and hot-water cornbread was a staple in everyone's household. I thought food stamps were a common currency that people valued from all races and socio-economic backgrounds.

It wasn't until my Uncle Ronnie, who was known for his brash and condescending disposition, began teasing me and taking great pride in calling me a welfare recipient that I began to realize those food stamps were viewed as a handicap or a detriment to my character. If his piercing words were meant to make me question my self-worth and identity as a young black girl, he accomplished his goal. Over the years, we have both laughed as we've reminisced about his insensitive remarks, but somehow in the midst of our laughter, the thought of his derogatory comments no longer appealed to me. As those words began to slowly sink into my head and I began to feel the emotional sting that resulted from them, the laughter that numbed my pain suddenly seemed to resurrect it.

Being poor and living in the inner- city projects of Louisville, KY as a child with my mother and siblings influenced how I perceived my capabilities and potential. However, it did not rob me of the fun I often had with neighborhood friends. Playing outside felt like a gift that was wrapped in lots of love. When my mother would grant me the permission to play outside after school, I was overjoyed. I was beyond excited because you never knew what type of characters you might run into. Would it be Charley, who was physically disabled and wandered through the projects aimlessly searching for someone to listen to his action packed and imaginative stories? Would it be old Nilly Willy, the neighborhood drunk, begging for money to buy his next "fix" to heal his pains and solve his problems? Or, would it be one of my school bullies eagerly waiting to pounce on my skinny and defenseless body? Either way, each day was an adventure. I was ready for whatever it brought my way. The feeling was intoxicating.

It was the closest thing to imagining I had won the Golden Ticket to attend Willy Wonka's Chocolate Factory except there wasn't a white man with an eccentric personality wearing a top hot and holding a cane to greet my friends and I. He wasn't there to welcome us into a world of wonderment to cultivate a colorful and excitable imagination. We had to create our own. This way of thinking sparked a sense of creativity that was harmless and often rooted in childhood innocence. However, you wouldn't be a kid if you didn't test the water or challenge the status quo; that's what makes life exciting and unpredictable, right?

I remember the day I felt the urge to explore the mischievous nature of being an eight-year old child. I was tempted to see if what I perceived to be happy and joyous outside could be escalated to even greater heights. Not thinking how my decision or pursuit of happiness would impact someone else, I accepted the invitation.

Unbeknownst to me an opportunity would present itself sooner than I could have imagined. Being that we lived in the first apartment to the projects we were especially close to the bus stop and shopping center. It was common to see residents and random people passing our front porch on their way to either one of those destinations. I guess you can say, if you couldn't afford to buy a TV, the view from the front porch was the next best thing, and sometimes even better.

On this particular day, as I sat on our front porch, I noticed a girl passing by. Even more so, I noticed that she had a five-dollar bill in her hand. Well, I knew I had a one-dollar bill, and after doing some mental math, I within seconds knew that hers was worth more. I suddenly thought of all the candy and goodies I could buy. So, what did I do? I convinced her that my one dollar bill was worth more. Being that she was a little younger she bought into my idea and just like magic, I had the golden ticket, or so I thought.

I immediately took the money and hid it in some weeds beneath the front step of our porch. I then proceeded to locate my brother so that I could confide in him what I had done. My gut feeling told me that I had done something wrong, but telling my brother made me feel better. After all, my mother did teach us right from wrong, and I did know the difference. Apparently, so did the girl's mother. Within minutes, there was a knock at our door. The persistent and sharp knock which echoed up our flight of steel steps guaranteed that my mother would awaken from her nap. I knew that she had little tolerance for this type of behavior and there was going to be hell to pay if she found out.

My brother and I stood there looking at one another with an overwhelming sense of fear and great anticipation. My heart began to pound, my skinny and weak legs began to betray me as I started pacing the living room floor. I felt as if I was more present than I ever had been, noticing every movement and sound. As the knock continued to get louder, I heard the words, "Who is that knocking at the door?" Once she made it to the living room, where my brother and I stood overwhelmed by fear, I'm sure the frightened and regretful look on our faces told her more than our words ever could. "Did one of yaw do something wrong?" I suddenly felt as if I was on trial and being interrogated except I was voiceless. At that moment, I wanted to be anywhere other than an arm's reach from my mother. I was smart enough to know that the further I stood away from her the better. Frustrated with our prolonged silence and in an obvious agitated state of mind, she proceeded to answer the door.

Forced to awaken from her nap and now ready to learn what I had done, I knew it was going to add more fuel to the fire. The lady at the door said words to the effect of "I sent my daughter to the store and she come back tellin' me she didn't have enough money because your daughter took her money. I want my money back!" My mother gave me a look that made me feel so small, to the point of wanting to disappear. "Did you take her money?" Before I could force an answer out of my dry and tasteless mouth, I heard this quiet and timid voice say, "She put the money in the grass by the front porch." My heart sank. I felt helpless and betrayed. I don't know if he thought he needed to fulfill his moral obligation as a five year old to do the right thing, or if he was terrified of being part of the wrath that was about to take place. I think we can both agree that neither of us wanted anything to do with a good ol' fashioned butt-whipping.

My mother decided to adhere to her usual tactics for punishment. A belt was her preferred way of handling misbehavior. Needless to say, that was the worst butt whipping I had ever received, even to this day. Not even Willy Wonka could have saved me from Mama's wrath. She probably would have whipped him too, if he'd had gotten in her way.

I learned something that day. I learned the importance of having compassion for others, regardless of what you have or don't have. I learned that when you take something that doesn't belong to you, it's not what you take that bears the most consequence, it's the humanity you take from others and yourself that matters most. We must consider others in our pursuit of happiness. There would be times when our paths would cross. Neither of us seemed to have any interest in discussing what had previously transpired. Fortunately for me she seemed to want to forget about that moment as much as I did. I wish I could say the same for my mother.

Seek the Humanity in Others as You Seek Happiness for Yourself

In Western society, the idea that you can have what you desire as long as you work hard and perform well is so rooted in the fibers of our society that we are systemically and intrinsically conditioned to not believe anything otherwise. As a result, this belief has cultivated a mindset of entitlement and self-serving attitudes that further validate the mentality of, "I see what I want, and I am going to get it." I am a strong advocate for self-sufficiency, a relentless drive, and have admiration for those who seize opportunities to bring their hopes and dreams to reality. The problem arises when what you want infringes upon someone else's beliefs or physical space to the point where someone has been violated at the expense of your need or negligence.

Consequently, your infringement is not rooted in an authentic reality of resilience. Being that you have to "rob Peter to pay Paul," you being Paul, in some way, shape or form relegates you to a position that undermines your power. You may think you have won the battle, you may think you have secured your title, or you may think you have restored your confidence and courage. What you may not realize is that it's a false victory. It's an illusion that has the potential to perpetuate social injustice, racial inequality and environmental disasters, to say the least.

When you unjustly defeat someone in a way where their voice is silenced, their hands are metaphorically tied and their pain is at the expense of your insensitive ways, your perceived resilience is likely to be temporary. When you do wrong at the expense of others, I believe the universe has a way of remembering your selfish deeds. It has a way of reminding you of what you did so that you have an opportunity to make your wrongs right. The question is, will you be ready? I believe the universe wants to hold us accountable for our actions, not necessarily to punish us, but to give us an opportunity to learn from our mistakes. This way, our resilience will manifest from a place that is not self-serving.

To prevent self-serving actions, it's essential to recognize and embrace your moral standards. Your standards create boundaries that guide and influence your decisions. It supports your belief system so that your actions are a reflection of your values and voice. It manages your negative thoughts by keeping you on a path that leads to a respectable and mutual understanding. Needless to say, if you have no standards, you are destined to have no peace.

I believe when we fail to adhere to a moral standard, we allow ourselves to erode our sense of compassion and judgement. This cripples our ability to have an appreciation and respect for others in our pursuit of happiness, which I feel everyone deserves, yet it needs to be attained without the baggage that could come along with it. To minimize conflict and to develop a greater understanding of your influence on others, answer the following questions:

- Are your goals and aspirations grounded with integrity and empathy?
- Can you sleep at night knowing that your success elevated the lives of others rather than encroached on their rights to be seen or heard?
- Do you take into consideration the feelings and values of others before making decisions that could be detrimental to their well-being?

I find it rather interesting the paradox as it relates to feeling self-deserving and our human desires to want more, be more, and do more. As children, we are taught to avoid taking what isn't ours, to show patience and gratitude and to respect our elders. Yet, as we become adults, the inclination to do "the right thing" seems to lose its pull and is reduced to a cliché that is as worn out as childhood hand-me-downs. I suggest that we all take a look in the mirror and re-evaluate our performance to see if we can identify potential areas in our lives where we are not only coming up short, but also selling someone else short. Where are we overlooking others by under-appreciating their value and what they have to offer as a result of keeping our eyes on the prize?

If you find that you are amongst those who engage in this behavior, learn to see yourself for who you really are by becoming aware of your influence on others. Sometimes it simply means connecting the dots and reflecting on your own life and understanding how your hurt has impacted others. There is an old saying, "Hurt people, hurt people." It's amazing how four small words can mean so much. It implies that when people are hurting, that pain is transferred to someone else in a way that causes some form of pain, whether it be physical, emotional, or psychological. This pain is a result of past wounds that have yet to be addressed and therefore remain unhealed. Think about it; how can you possibly build a rapport and connect with others in a way that conveys a sense of emotional stability and well-being if you are still suffering and battling your own demons? When you are hurting, in some form or another, that pain will show up and be present in your daily performances. It's these performances that dictate how you build bridges to others to create healthy and sustainable relationships.

Self-Awareness Breeds Self-Compassion

In the pursuit of your happiness, if you are not willing to take a deep dive into your past traumas, trials, and tribulations to reveal the root of your pain, you will continue to create emotional barriers and conflicts between yourself and others. In addition, you may find that you put yourself first at the expense of others even when they may have your best interests in mind. Or, you may engage in a perpetual cycle of dysfunction that has the potential to stunt your growth. The dysfunction can materialize in your language, verbal and non-verbal, which negatively contributes to your ability to rise and deliver your best performance. Therefore, I want to encourage you to stop hurting and start healing so that in the pursuit of your happiness, you see beyond the scope of your life, but also into the lives of others.

Now, just to be clear, I believe it is noteworthy to emphasize the difference between pursuing your goals in spite of those who consciously try to prevent you from becoming the best version of yourself, and those who are innocent bystanders who happen to get in the crossfire of your ambitions. Here is the difference: When I talk about hurting other people, I am not talking about those who will get emotionally bruised as a result of the changed dynamics of your relationship and as a byproduct of the pursuit of your goals.

Quite naturally, when you pursue any endeavor with all of your being, it's rather difficult, yet necessary, for you to perform differently. This causes your relationships to be impacted in one way or another. In this case, it is normal and expected that some people may feel hurt, left out and temporarily forgotten about in the process. If this happens, just know that it's okay. Those who genuinely care about you will always allow you to be yourself. They understand that this is temporary and as a result they are willing to go the distance with you.

As you grow into a stronger, wiser, more resilient you, those who are not on the same transformational journey may perceive you as

I want to encourage you to stop hurting and start healing
so that in the pursuit of your happiness, you see beyond the
scope of your life, but also into the lives of others.

a threat to their identity, which was in the making long before you entered their world. Therefore, by no means should you hold yourself accountable for the ways in which people manifest their fears as a result of your achievements. You must develop the flexibility and self-confidence to become unapologetic when it comes to putting yourself first and living the fullest life possible. It's also important to note that those who really care about you will understand the sacrifices and struggles that you will endure to rise and step into your greatness.

People Who Genuinely Care Seek No Apology

Those who genuinely care about you are less likely to question your intentions, because they know the inspiration and passion that fuels them. They tend to be flexible and more giving because the fire that burns within you is the same fire they seek for themselves. Yes, at times it may seem as if they are getting the short end of the stick. For instance, when you feel as though you need to protect and economize your time due to prior obligations and as a result you have less time to spend with them. However, the reality is they are receiving less of you at times, and you wouldn't accomplish much if they didn't. Or, you may find that someone wants you to compromise your integrity to fulfill their wants and needs at the expense of your own. You can't please everyone, nor should you try. Any attempt to please others in your pursuit of happiness will inevitably have an unsatisfying and predictable ending. It's like watching a bad movie you wished you never invested time in. Not only did it waste your time, there was nothing valuable to take away from it that would further advance your life.

In contrast, carelessly hurting someone while in your pursuit of happiness is wrong and should be avoided. Anyone with a sense of integrity and compassion for other human beings will naturally take others into consideration as they maneuver towards attaining their goals. When hurt people hurt people, unfortunately, their pain can be too great to recognize the pain or humanity in others, which further alienates those on the receiving end. Their pain seems to mask the ability to "read" others. Whatever they are going through or have gone through has left such an impression on their psyche that they can't seem to see or move beyond the plight of their circumstance. Why? Because the pain follows them like a shadow on a hot humid day, stalking their every move, hiding behind every twist and turn they encounter. You don't always realize it's there, but it is. It's for this reason that the depth of your hurt and suffering can be seen and felt by others, especially when you are not conscious of your feelings and the impact they have on your life.

Unfortunately, growing up in what appeared to be a loving yet dysfunctional family, I witnessed many examples of family members blatantly hurt and disrespected one another to the point of physical violence. This left me to wonder what could possibly be going on in that person's life to make them want to say and do these types of mean spirited acts to a loved one? It wasn't until years later, I realized that the person committing the act is likely to be in even more pain than they are causing the other person. Rather than talk through their feelings and emotions as adults, the situation instantly escalates to a level of physical harm.

Some people want to be heard and validated for their thoughts and feelings and when they feel as if their point of view is threatened, they might lack the emotional maturity to handle the situation appropriately. They would rather be right and cause harm than be wrong and consider another point of view in their pursuit of their happiness. It's a performance that is truly difficult to watch yet they aim to take center stage in hopes to garner applause for what they consider to be a victory at the expense of another family member.

It's as if they seek a standing ovation to confirm their actions or the justification of their wrongdoing. However, I believe even the most committed theater-goer would find this performance distasteful and a waste of time at the very least. No one wants to witness the injustice of another, especially at the expense of someone de-humanizing and degrading someone else because they lack a moral compass or personal boundaries. And the Oscar goes to…I don't think so!

Time to Rise and Shine!

- ### Empathize with Others

  The ability to understand the experiences and stories of others first begins with your willingness to empathize with others. When you are generous with your humanity by allowing yourself to see through the eyes of others, you take part in something much bigger than yourself.

  Empathy is that "something" that allows you to show compassion for others regardless of their cultural background, religious affiliation, and intellectual capacity. It's what facilitates spiritual and emotional healing within yourself and for others. Author and researcher Brene Brown once said, "We are hardwired to connect with others; it's what gives purpose and meaning to our lives, and without it there is suffering."

  You empathize with others by connecting your stories to theirs. When you intentionally seek commonality rather than differences between one another it naturally creates a sense of unity and understanding. Why? Because you don't seek to judge or justify the existence or position in the life of others; rather you seek to validate and give voice to the existence and position in others. There is a difference.

- *Become an Active Listener*

  Active Listening requires you to not only listen with your ears, but even more so, with your whole being. It's having the ability to listen with your eyes by giving people the attention necessary to not only feel heard, but also seen. It's your ability to listen with your heart by demonstrating and embracing your compassion for others. When people see that you care, they know you are listening.

  Active listening also allows you to retrieve additional information that you would not have otherwise. It allows you to listen to the subtext, the feelings and emotions beneath the words to get a more accurate assessment of one's thoughts and ideas. It helps you to see people for who they really are without making assumptions based on what was heard. It's been said that, "actions speak louder than words." Therefore, when you engage in active listening look for contradictions, misaligned words and actions that don't appear to be grounded in truth.

- *Ask For Feedback*

  One of the easiest things to do when considering others in your pursuit of happiness is to simply ask the right questions. Sometimes when we infringe on others' rights it's simply because we didn't take their point of view or values into consideration. We didn't bother to understand where they are in their journey of life: what have they been through, what are they going through, or where are they trying to go. However, when we take the time to ask, we see more than just the person—we see their humanity. As a result, we are able to connect the dots and ask the right questions.

  The questions are more effective when you choose you-focused rather than I-focused questions. They could be asked in a way in which the other person feels as if you are looking out for their best interest and that you truly care. For example, are you satisfied with the resolution to this problem and if not, why? Or, your voice matters. What do you want me to know or do to minimize the communication gap that exists between the two of us? Your questions should not cause people to doubt and question you. When they begin to question your intentions or motivations, it is a sign you have asked the wrong questions. Therefore, let your questions come from the heart. Let them manifest from a place where only love, compassion, and empathy reside. When you do, people are more likely to respond favorably.

Let the questions you ask advance the conversation forward. This will allow you to progress constructively to gaining a better understanding of their world and how you could potentially impact it as a result of pursuing your goals. It's when we focus on the wrong questions time gets wasted, problems get stalled, and people get hurt. Therefore, be efficient in your questions; your relationships and success depend on it.

- ## Develop A Win/Win Mentality

When you are winning in the game of life, it's just as important to be aware of who is losing as a result of your success. As people, we are conditioned to win. It's what helps to develop our self-worth and gives us a sense of validation. It's what makes us feel as if we have a place in the world simply because we have earned our right to be here. However, when we spend too much time relishing in our success without acknowledging the struggles and injustices we may have imposed on others, we must ask, are we really winning?

To have a win/win mentality, allow yourself to be aware of the wants and needs of the other person. When you understand their wants and needs by actively listening, it's only then that you can give them something of value to make it a win/win situation. If you give someone something and they have no use for it, then it has no value. If it has no value then it has little meaning. As a result, people will not be inspired to buy into your ideas or invest in a relationship. They want to know, what's in it for me?

It is essential that your win/win mentality is rooted in fairness. As the saying goes, what comes around goes around. Learn to treat people the way you would want to be treated. When you do, it becomes a win for you because your integrity becomes an asset to your personal brand and character. People will recognize the good in who you are, but also the good in what you do. When you seek to win, think bigger than yourself. When you come to the conclusion that a shared win is better than a "My win," that's when everyone wins.

Chapter 2

RISE UP TO SPEAK UP

Stand before the people you fear and speak your mind
—even if your voice shakes.
Maggie Kuhn

My father was my hero. His super power was his ability to outshine the sun to light up my world. When he was around, he made my day so bright I would become blinded to his flaws and only see the best of who he was. Needless to say, the light and joy that he brought into my life represented so much promise and hope that the very thought of him made my heart swell. No one could replace him, not even one of our home town heroes.

I distinctly remember the day my father took me to Central Park in Louisville, Kentucky for an outdoor event. As we arrived, I noticed the park was unusually occupied with an enormous amount of people. At the time, I couldn't make sense of it, not realizing my curiosity would soon be satisfied. There he was, the man so many people from around the world adored. He was pure beauty as he stood taking autographs from his determined and awestruck fans.

He was one of the most handsome black men I had ever seen. His skin appeared flawless and unscathed despite his profession and often brash showmanship. He was larger than life. He was the one and only heavy weight boxing champion, Muhammad Ali. Yet, despite the magnitude of his success, in my eyes, he couldn't compare to my father. It's for this reason I was overtaken by silence when I received the phone call that my father wanted me to come and live with him.

Words could not express the feelings I felt inside. What I do know is that I was filled to the brim with excitement as I anxiously paced the floor anticipating the moment I would arrive in Minnesota. Let's just say, my imagination was far from betraying me. My imagination was overwhelmingly rich with visions of tender and priceless moments, moments that I usually only witnessed on TV. I knew then it was a good chance I would reap the benefits of being my father's only child. I knew that I was more likely to get the benefit of the doubt, the last piece of sweet potato pie and, most importantly, more love and affection.

After arriving in Minnesota, I remember dropping a gallon of milk on the kitchen floor and expecting to be reprimanded, but those thoughts were the furthest from the truth. I was simply asked to clean it up and then proceeded to go on with my day. "Are you kidding me?" I thought, "Life can't be this easy, or can it?" This was a new way of living and I loved it. The fact that it wasn't powdered milk from the government was already a win for me. Just like the Jeffersons, I was movin' on up. The only problem was my father didn't have a deluxe apartment in the sky like the family on the TV show *The Jeffersons*.

Being that my father was single with no other children, he lived in a one-bedroom apartment. He got the bed in the bedroom and I got the living room couch. This would be the first time I felt cheated by my father, but not the last. After sleeping on the couch for over a year, one night I decided I had had enough. I wanted a change. It never dawned on me that sleeping in my father's bed was wrong or could potentially jeopardize our relationship and ultimately my quality of life. He had always made me feel safe and protected. I believe I subconsciously thought, why would this be any different? The next thing I knew, I acted on my impulses and made the decision to sleep in my father's bed. I don't even know if he knew that I was there. All I knew was that I was at peace and within minutes had fallen asleep.

It was common to be awakened by the sound of my father saying, "Rise and shine! However, this particular morning I had no idea I would be awakened to something that would ultimately change my life. This particular morning something was different. I was always awakened by the sound of his voice, but never by the touch of his hands. The same hand that once cradled me in his arms when I was a baby. The same hand that hugged me tirelessly after his return from the military. The same hand that possibly picked up the phone to call and say I love you.

When his hand touched me in a place that I knew was off limits to him and the rest of the world, it was as if I became frozen in time. I felt as if I couldn't move or breathe. I was afraid, confused and disappointed all at the same time. The only words that were spoken was him telling me to go to the bathroom to clean up. What just happened I thought? Why did he feel as if he needed to go to that place? A place that was sacred. A place that I was still in the process of getting to know. I knew a boundary had been crossed. The question was, what was I going to do about it?

Soon after coming from the bathroom I went to the living room and sat on the couch. I felt as if my world had just come tumbling down. As I sat on the couch, my mind began to race wondering what I should do and who I should tell. Before I could come to a conclusion, I suddenly heard his voice call out "Donna" repeatedly. Donna was his girlfriend. It was obvious to me that he wanted me to believe that I was mistaken for her. Although I was 11-years old, I knew better.

Somehow, I got up enough courage to get off the couch and tell my father what was on my mind. Little did I know, he was well ahead of me. As I stood in the living room facing the front door, there he stood. I immediately told him that I wanted to call my grandmother and go home.

To my surprise, my father pulled a gun from behind his back and told me that if I told he would kill himself. The situation escalated well beyond my control. In that moment I felt hopeless and my family, who was hundreds of miles away, suddenly felt as if they were millions of miles away. The fear that I once felt had now completely overtaken my body. A body that no longer felt familiar. Just as my mind was distant so was the connection to my body. My eyes welled with tears. My heart began to pound ferociously as every moment was heightened with great anticipation. Now that he knows that I want to go home, will he decide to kill me too? As he made his way back to his room, I frantically dashed to the couch. A couch which I had just abandoned to sleep in my father's bed had suddenly become my safe haven and my refuge. There was no way I was going back to sleep. There was no way I was going to allow this to happen again. I kept my eyes open, but because I was afraid, I kept my mouth shut. At least until I was in a space where I felt safe to share my feelings.

One night after being dropped off at my father's friend's house something in me said that it was a good time to share what had happened. However, before I could get a word out of my mouth it was apparent she sensed something was wrong. My conversation was different. It was shallow and brief. My attention span was short as my eyes seem to dart with fear moment by moment. I gravely anticipated my father knocking on the door to take me home and apparently it showed. When she asked me what was wrong, it was then I told her what had happened. Being that she was a member of our church and had a daughter roughly my age, I felt safe to confide in her what had happened. The next thing I knew, my father came to pick me up. I could tell by the look on his face and fear in his eyes, he knew I had told. Needless to say, I had no idea that would be the last night I would spend at my father's apartment.

The next day, I went to school and before the day was over, I was escorted out of class. I eventually went and stayed in a group home until my mother came to Minnesota to get me. That was the first time I experienced living with white people. They were good to me. They let me listen and dance to Michael Jackson's songs, which I loved. His music definitely helped to take my mind off my father. After approximately two weeks I went to the airport to meet my mother. I so desperately wanted to see her. As people exited the plane, I couldn't get to her fast enough. Then in a sea of strangers there she was, a beautiful, classy black woman in her imitation brown fur coat wearing one of her most stylish wigs. Yep, that was my mama.

Somehow, my father found his way to the airport. I'm not sure how he knew the details of my arrangements, but I do know that he tried to convince my mother to let me stay. My mother was not entertaining much of what he had to say. I'm also sure that if she had come home without me there would have been hell to pay with my grandparents. That would be the last time I saw my father until he came to Louisville to visit a few years later.

I believe the experience I had with my father caused me to lose part of who I was that day. I lost faith in humanity and part of my childhood innocence that I could never get back. However, I did gain something very important: my voice. By speaking up, I discovered an inner power and strength I never knew I had. It was the ability to advocate for myself by realizing the importance of not protecting others in a time of crisis, but protecting myself. My words may have opened their ears, but I am proud of the fact that it opened my mouth. As I reflect on that moment, I see a girl who was afraid and feared for the worst, but was able to rise and reclaim her voice and it's because of that voice she is the speaker she is today.

Your Voice Matters and So Do You

A powerless voice is destined to lead you to a powerless state of being. It is for this reason why one of the most important tasks you will ever encounter during your lifetime will be to find and embrace your authentic voice. It's what distinguishes you from other people so that you can be seen and appreciated for who you really are.

It's an expression of you that is cultivated through authenticity and your willingness to be forthcoming in your thoughts and ideas. It allows your contributions to humanity to be grounded in originality, causing people to recognize the various shades of your personality, the depth of your values, and the strength of your convictions.

Your voice, when used with power and passion, is what people cling to when they are searching for hope. In such cases, your voice becomes the anchor to their unstable and unpredictable lives. It grounds them in a way that broadens their horizons and gives them the inspiration to live with purpose. As a result, your voice then has a way of sparking new interests by removing the mental veil that has overshadowed their brightest ideas.

Whether you realize it or not, the world is starving to hear your voice. People want to be liberated from their burdens in life. They want to be entertained with your humor and storytelling abilities, to be enlightened and engaged. They want to be transported from their daily struggles to a place where they can re-imagine new possibilities and soar to new heights. So you see, your voice has value.

Those who are not able to see the value in their voice are those who deprive themselves of the necessary components to maximize it. Therefore, to maximize your voice means you are willing to nurture it. Nurturing requires you to own your voice by being unapologetic about the things you feel strongly about. It means you are not walking on eggshells to voice your concerns or deepest regrets, but rather share them in a way that is a representation of your values and beliefs.

Just like a plant needs to be nurtured for proper growth and development, so does your voice. For instance, your voice needs a platform to express itself regardless of how big or small. It needs you to show up with confidence so that you can operate from your highest point of being to speak your truth. In addition, your voice should not be easily compromised in the face of fear.

Your voice is at its best when you know what your purpose is and you are not afraid to act on it. When you know what your purpose is, your voice is then strengthened as a result of it. Your voice now has something to fight for. It is now being channeled in a way that creates a focus and intentionality with what you say and how you say it. Therefore, you are less likely to meander with your words. They are grounded in power and precision.

Fear Has a Way of Silencing Your Voice—Don't Let It

Unfortunately, although our voices have value, we don't always use them to the best of our abilities. We somehow let our fears get in the way of expressing our opinions with candor and honesty. We let our fears minimize the power of our voice while choosing words that tend to undermine them. By selecting words that have a tendency to "soften the blow," our words carry less impact. They become watered down with insignificant meaning, potentially robbing you of your assertiveness and influence.

This can happen particularly when we try to avoid conflict, yet conflict can be the very thing that allows us to live our best lives.

According to Mike Robbins, author of *be yourself*, "The Chinese symbol for conflict is a great reminder to all of us about the true nature of conflict. The first character in the symbol represents 'danger' while the second one represents 'opportunity.'" Therefore it is advantageous to you when you understand and accept the power of your voice at the expense of your fears. Conflict can make you run or, if you're willing to face your fears, it can allow you to move mountains to see the glorious opportunities that await you.

Fear has a way of diminishing you to people pleasing. The interesting part about diminishing your language to "people please" is that you also diminish yourself in the process. Although you consciously or subconsciously play down your thoughts and ideas to perhaps build someone up, you simultaneously sacrifice your true voice. Consequently, they only see and hear a fraction of the person you are capable of being. Another reason why we don't utilize our voice to its fullest potential is because we don't know its potential.

Our potential has a way of hiding among the shallow words that are designed to protect us. It hides behind the self-limiting thoughts that perpetuate self-doubt and insecurity. As a result, the safe haven which we've created for ourselves that keeps us bound with fear doesn't allow us to rise with a sense of self-knowing. It forces you to surrender and retreat to your comfort zone, preventing you from experiencing the breakthrough needed to challenge your voice.

When you challenge your voice you acknowledge it for what it is. You don't make excuses. You look for pitfalls that disrupt your ability to be an effective communicator, whether it's through your words or actions. You look for inconsistencies that don't add up. Particularly when your voice is not meeting the demand of the moment. For instance, if you are in a situation that calls for your honesty yet you find it difficult to express yourself in a way that is grounded in truth, ask yourself questions to boost your awareness:

- Why is my voice out of alignment with my expectations, and what can I do to change it?

- Does my voice seem to diminish around certain individuals, and if so, why?

- When I am not speaking in my authentic voice, who am I protecting and why?

Furthermore, challenge your voice by surrounding yourself with other individuals who seem to have little problem challenging their own. Let the power behind their voices inspire you to speak up and speak out. Be in the moment, and let their voices resonate with you so that you identify with words that seem to have the greatest impact. Therefore, listen for power words that elevate the conversation and force you to think and act differently.

If you can, find a way to emulate their voice without duplicating their voice. Emulating gives you a blueprint and lays the foundation for an empowered voice without compromising its integrity. However, if you duplicate, you are no longer in a position to express your individuality. Your individuality becomes non-existent because who you were has now become consolidated with who they are. Needless to say, the essence of your voice no longer conveys your unique qualities and is now a commodity with little value.

Finally, you can challenge your voice by sharing who you are with others. When you use your voice in a way that allows people to get a deeper sense of who you are, you are essentially sharing what could be considered as information below the waterline. Mike Robbins, the author of *be yourself*, uses the metaphor of an iceberg to highlight this concept. He says, "What it takes for us to live our lives, have relationships, and do our work at a deeper level of authenticity is for us to lower that waterline, share more of who we really are, and speak our truth courageously."

The benefits of using your voice to establish who you are and what you stand for is priceless. When you make the decision to show up and contribute your thoughts and ideas people tend to hold you in high esteem. As people, we understand the vulnerability that goes hand in hand with the freedom of personal expression.

A vulnerability has the potential to break you down or build you up depending on your degree of resilience in the midst of adversity. Regardless, people have an appreciation for those who are willing to risk relationships and opportunities to be heard, who are willing to be rejected in spite of the goodness of their heart or meaningful intentions.

When you allow yourself to rise and speak up you create an opportunity for human connection. Your voice has a way of bridging the gap between the hopeful and helpless or those who are perceived to be powerful and those who are powerless. Your voice serves as a conduit to unite and strengthen humanity so we can rise as a people rather than as individuals. As the saying goes, there is power in numbers.

Your Voice Has the Power to Change Lives

The more you use your voice the more chances you have to change lives and potentially the world. Amanda Gorman, the talented and amazing poet who delivered such a passionate and heartfelt poem at the 2021 presidential inauguration, is making an undeniable imprint on this world. She used her poetic voice and regal presence to captivate our imaginations. She inspired us to hope for a better future to not only "see the light, but to be the light." She showed us what grace under pressure looks like and what can be achieved when you are willing to step out on faith to rise and shine.

It was Amanda's courageous spirit and thought-provoking words that provided the fuel needed to unite the world. In spite of divisive rhetoric, historical wounds and current social injustice, she made a concerted effort to make a difference—and so she did. However, let's be honest. Sometimes the thought of changing the world with only our voices can seem like a daunting and overwhelming task. Consequently, sometimes in order to have an appreciation for things, we must normalize them and make them more relatable. How do you do that? You do that by first understanding the impact of your voice. You are not Amanda Gorman, nor should you aspire to be, but you are You!

Your voice is the hallmark to your identity. It's what certifies your uniqueness so that you can rise bravely to claim your stake in the world. It comes with a seal of approval meaning that no one needs to validate it. You are the creator. You set the tone and pace of your words, but even more so you set the rules. You get to decide when to hold back and when to let go. You get to choose if you want to maximize the lives of others by building them up or if you want to minimize their character by breaking them down. However, if you choose to take the high road, the road that contributes to the uprising of humanity, fosters hope and inspiration, your voice will have served its purpose.

Your voice is bigger than you. Your voice can liberate you and make you shine so that you can be seen as the star you truly are. It can unleash the greatness that lies within you in a way that allows you to speak on your purpose—your reason for existing. It's for this reason your voice should be embraced. Let the power of your voice nudge you in the back when you want to suppress it so that you can rise and shine to live out your potential. You are a voice in this world and you matter.

Your voice is the hallmark to your identity.
It's what certifies your uniqueness so that
you can rise bravely to claim your stake in the world.

Time to Rise and Shine!

- *Identify Things That Make You Feel Emotionally Charged*

  The things that make you cry and cause you to feel emotionally charged are a sign that you care. When you care about something that moves you and evokes a response from you then it's much easier to use your voice to defend it and protect it. You become naturally inclined to share your views and opinions as they relate to the things you are invested in. You become socially aware and develop a heightened sense of other people's words and actions because what brings you to tears create feelings of sensitivity and vulnerability.

  The next time you cry, ask yourself, why? For instance, if you are having a "bad day," truly understand the meaning behind those words. Are you having a bad day because someone said something that offended you or are you having a bad day not only because of their offensive words or actions, but because their words and actions are rooted in a broader context? It's context that gives your perception a deeper and more profound meaning. As a result, you stand a better chance of advocating for yourself and using your voice to be seen, and also to be heard.

- *Reflect on Your Skill Set and Self-Mastery*

  Think about the things you are truly good at. Those things that you feel you are able to do in your sleep. Or the things that you may take for granted yet other people seem to have a great deal of appreciation for. Whichever your answer may be, it's a good chance it's something that you have mastered. Having this skill set is not only an asset to your personal or professional development, but it is also an asset to your voice.

38

When you master something, it opens the door of opportunity for you to not only showcase your talents, but also to use your voice in a way that expresses your thoughts and ideas. It's your level of mastery and your ability to articulate it that enriches peoples' lives. It helps them to expand their limited view of the world and what it has to offer. Why? Because your voice qualifies you and allows people to potentially hear things that are above and beyond their intellectual understanding.

- *Reflect on Your Childhood Aspirations*
What did you want to be when you grew up? What was that thing that made your eyes smile and your soul sing when you thought about your future career? Our perception of who we aspire to be is connected to who we were born to be. Todd Henry, author of *Louder Than Words* says, "But those early days of wonder—the vast expanses of horizon that hinted at limitless possibility—can give us insight into the deeper seeds of fascination that still reside within us."

I believe that as a child there are seeds that are planted within us. They are simply waiting to be nurtured so that we can come into full bloom and blossom to our potential. However, as we transition from childhood into adulthood if those seeds are not nurtured and cultivated they lay dormant within the depths of our souls. Therefore, if you are still searching for your purpose in life don't get stuck with looking into the future thinking about what you could be. Look to your past so that you can be taken on an emotional journey and re-connect with your soul to become who you ought to be.

Chapter 3

GIVE BACK TO MOVE FORWARD

I've learned that you shouldn't go through life
with a catcher's mitt on both hands;
you need to be able to throw something back.
Maya Angelou

It was common for a church bus to ride through the projects on Wednesday evenings to take children to Bible study. I guess you can say it was the church's way of investing in our community by providing children the opportunity to develop a stronger relationship with the Lord. Even more so, to provide a safe haven from the hustle and bustle of the streets. I must say, it was not always easy to pull away from the fun I was having with my friends. However, at times the best fun was with me, myself, and I, whether I was roller skating, riding my bike or just climbing a tree. When I saw that bus, I knew it was time to go. To be quite honest, one of my motivations stemmed from the fact that I knew I was going to get a treat at church. I was always curious which kind it would be. As you can probably guess, I loved sugar. I was a junk food junkie and I had the cavities to prove it. However, years later I developed an appreciation of the church for investing their time by taking us children to Bible study.

Going to church allowed me the opportunity to sit on that bus and look at my environment from a different perspective. It literally provided me a vehicle to navigate through my neighborhood and see a world beyond my own despite my struggles. It allowed me to see people and things without being thrust in the midst of the noise. So, when I got on that bus and found my seat, I filled it up with every part of my being. I occupied our space as if I owned it. I relished every moment, especially since I knew I would be joined by another hopeful passenger within a matter of minutes.

It seemed with every bump in the road my body easily gave into the forceful bounces with an enthusiastic and animated gesture. I let my head bounce freely and body sway with the rhythm of the engine and the reverberation from the unexpected yet thrilling bumps. I felt alive and in the moment. Then came the day that I thought it would be a good time for me to reciprocate by showing them that their investment in me was recognized and appreciated.

My mother had a tendency for styling my hair with an air of style and sophistication at a young age. It was for this reason my first grade teacher and my classmates called me Ms. Piggy. Apparently, on the Muppet Show, Ms. Piggy wore different hair styles and needless to say everyone thought we had something in common. I didn't mind particularly since I received special attention that I probably wouldn't have received otherwise. Well, one particular Sunday morning, my mother invested extra time and patience in pressing my hair with a hot comb. This Sunday ritual was as common as the bus that would pick us up for Bible school. The only difference was that while church set my soul on fire, my mama, at times, made me feel like my head was on fire. Needless to say, it definitely wasn't my favorite thing to do, but at the time it seemed necessary to get the results my mother and I wanted. When she finished, I knew that if Ms. Piggy could have seen my hair, even she would have been proud. I guess you can say the anticipation of wondering if whether or not I was going to get burned by the hot comb subsided after I seen the results. It made me feel as if the discomfort was worth it.

Once I arrived at church and the pastor began his sermon, it wasn't long before I would have an opportunity to give back. So, what did I do? I volunteered to get baptized. At that moment, it seemed like the right thing to do, but little did I know my actions would prove to be the wrong thing to do, at least in my mother's eyes. When it came time for the pastor to dunk my head into that water, I was nervous, but I also thought I was doing the right thing and that my mother would be proud of me. I was going to be transformed into a new me. I wanted to be closer to God and getting baptized was the answer. You know where I'm headed with this, right? Well, after I got baptized and my head went under the water, nothing seemed to have changed. I felt the same as I had before I got baptized. However, I was cold and eager to change clothes. Then it dawned on me. As I began to dry myself off and change into dry clothes my hair was no longer smooth and silky. It wasn't laying down on my scalp quite like my mother had it. It managed to transform itself into something I feared- an afro!

My heart started to race, my eyes started to well, my thin bony legs started to nervously pace the floor. "Ewwww, my mama gonna kill me!" These were the words running through my now nappy head. I don't remember Ms. Piggy's hair looking like this. I would have remembered if she wore an afro and since I didn't, I didn't feel quite the same. I was beginning to feel as if I looked more like Kermit the Frog with an afro rather than the glamourous Ms. Piggy. When I finally saw my mother, it was obvious she felt the same way. I have to say, that moment resulted in a day that I will never forget.

The look on her face and the tone of her voice left such an impression in my mind that when I got older, I thought twice before

I got baptized again. I knew that God had my back, but I was afraid that my mother would have my butt, if you know what I mean. I also thought about and questioned what I gained from trying to give back. Was giving back an opportunity at the expense of "getting into trouble?" Was it supposed to teach me a lesson that I would eventually regret? Or was it simply overrated and got more credit than it truly deserved? Little did I know, there would be another opportunity to give back

My grandmother was a hardworking and God-fearing woman who was as round and plump as the watermelons she'd share with her grandchildren on a hot summer day. Although she worked herself tirelessly, she had a heart of gold. She worked hard every day at a local hospital in the housekeeping department for many years. Despite never being paid what she truly deserved, she never forgot the importance of giving back.

When I was a child, she would often tell me about her dysfunctional childhood. A childhood that was plagued with emotional scars and painful memories. However, I believe it was her childhood riddled with experiences that fueled her determination to become such a loving and generous spirit. I also believe it's why she had such high hopes and expectations for me. Being that she didn't volunteer in the traditional sense, meaning outside the home, she made it a priority to see to it that I volunteered at the same hospital she had become enslaved to.

Initially, I questioned her motives. I said to myself, "I'm black, and poor. I get a welfare check for $140.00 a month that barely covers food and expenses to and from school. I wear second- hand clothes. I cash in pop bottles for bus fare. Grandmamma raised her children in the projects, my mother raised her children in the projects and I'm probably going to raise my children in the projects and she wants me to volunteer?" But, I knew that my grandmother wasn't crazy so I decided to give it a try.

Volunteering at the information desk gave me a sense of purpose. It was the first time in my life I remember feeling as if I was somebody and that I could make a difference in the world. The uniform I wore gave me a sense of belonging and that was something I was proud of. I walked with my head held high, I strutted as if I had a pocket full of money, but most importantly, I forgot about my run-down shoes, and the dinginess of my socks, because the moment I was asked for assistance from a woman who had just walked in the emergency room with a child limp in her arms saying, "This child has just been molested. Where do I take him?" I knew my life would never be the same. As I looked at that child, in many ways it was as if I was looking at myself. I could see the fear in his eyes as he searched for answers, peace, and protection from the madness that had just transpired. As if he was trying to make sense of a world that neglected to protect him.

After giving back, I now realize how much was given to me. As I gave my heart and time, what I received in return was priceless. For instance, the opportunity to give strengthened my confidence and resilience. It helped me to see that I wasn't alone in my struggles and that everyone has a story. It just so happened that the little boy gave me a chance to help him as someone had helped me and for that I am grateful. I am also grateful to have had an opportunity to share a poem titled "Glory Be To God," which I was honored to recite at my grandmother's funeral. Once again, I felt as if I had a chance to give back to her by reminding those in attendance exactly why she made a difference.

Glory Be To God

As a child, anxious and eager, I would run to the alley at my grandmama's house. Barefoot, hair nappy as the lint on my worn hand-me-downs. My eyes begin to search the narrow confines of the alley.
"Where is that lady in blue?" my mind began to question.
But I first must bypass the distractions of roaming dogs and cats, maybe a staggering drunk or two, trash that city workers have yet to claim, and kids ranging from the unruly to the unwanted as they are unified by play and the hunger of laughter.

The longer I wait the more my head gets consumed with self-doubt and hints of frustration. As my head begins to fall from the weight of boredom and the history of undeserving disappointment, I become resurrected, restored in my faith, and renewed by the sight of my grandmother. She stands too far to hear my cry, but I say to myself, "Glory be to God."

I begin to run with each foot smacking the hot and worn pavement. So excited that I could hardly contain and navigate my thin fragile body. I run so fast I feel as if I am floating in the air, meeting the birds in the heavens and going up a yonder to meet my Lord way before my time while escaping the glass and debris that awaits my return.

The closer I get to her, she becomes as picturesque as the realism paintings of Albert Edelfelt, William Bliss Baker or Gustave Courbet capturing the simplicities of nature, the strength of her backbone, the sway in her walk, the contours of her face defining and revealing her struggles, fortitude, the mountains that she's climbed and the valleys which she's had to cross. As we meet, my arms embrace her plump waist not able to fully go around they rest on her hips, which carried the nine babies she birthed and some of the grandchildren, which she raised. As I meet her tired and restless eyes, I say to myself, "Glory be to God."

We walk hand in hand as we discuss the day's events. Inside, my heart begins to feel saddened because I can foresee the disappointment, which will occupy and infiltrate her eyes as we reach our final destination called home. Food yet to be prepared and the house unrecognizable since the early hours of which she left. But I smile, because I realize that I am in the presence of a queen. A queen who was never adorned with the crown that she so deserved, a queen who was loved but at times didn't always have the support from her royal court to lift her up when she needed a helping hand. But today, I ask you, did she need a crown? Which is nothing more than a material possession that is symbolic of wealth and power and solidifies one's self or position within a social hierarchy. What does it all matter, when you have faith in God?

It was because of her faith that she was able to dodge the many daggers that came her way. I've witnessed her tears, my heart has felt her pain, my lips have mimicked her songs of praise, my ears have heard her cries and when she was too tired to defend herself she would often times say, "say no more," and through it all I only imagine having an ounce of the strength and courage which she possessed.

Today it is my hope that her legacy as a grandmother will live for generations to come. She represents so much more than the numbers on her paycheck before retiring, the broken and unstable home where she dwelled, the stench of alcohol that lingered from her belongings despite never consuming it.

She represented sacrifice, struggle, giving when there was little to give, resiliency after a storm, forgiveness when she was pushed up against a wall, determination when trying to keep her family out of harm's way. She was my shero.

The morals and values she instilled in me as a child are reflective of me standing before you today. However, I pray that someday when I am laying in a casket someone will be standing before you speaking on my behalf and the legacy that I've left behind. Oh, if I could be so lucky because in the end that's what we want to know, right? Did we really matter? Did we really make a difference? Well, if you knew her story, her beginning, middle, and end, you would know the answer to that question.

As I continue my journey in life and face adversity and battles that may cause me to weaken and fall to my knees, I will think of my grandmother and draw strength from the life that she lived and I will say to myself, "Glory be to God."

Embrace the Importance of Giving Back

In a society where success is often measured by what you have rather than what you do, it reinforces the notion that the way in which you help others determines how people perceive you. Thankfully, people's perceptions have the potential to establish discord between what is perceived as valuable and what really matters. This ideology is commonly reflected in our culture by prioritizing trivial goods and services to become more of a necessity than an option. However, it is ultimately our responsibility as people to distinguish between the two and understand the benefits to helping others in spite of societal norms or cultural tendencies.

Giving back to move forward is truly more than a selfless act of kindness or a good deed. Additionally, its effects are more far-reaching and influential than what appears on the surface. On a deeper level, it facilitates the advancement of society, promotes self-esteem, provides a vehicle for people to demonstrate their gratitude to those who've helped pave the way for their success, expands your knowledge base, and contributes to the upward mobility of those in need of support. Furthermore, giving back or volunteering has prominent health benefits that should not be ignored or underestimated. For instance, according to the Mayo Clinic Health Systems, "volunteering decreases the risk of depression, gives people a sense of purpose, reduces stress levels, helps people to live longer, and helps you meet others and develop new relationships." It's these reasons and more why we should be inspired to help one another regardless of social and economic status, race, gender, age, and religious affiliation.

When you don't allow yourself to give back to those who not only have paved the way for your success but who could simply use a helping hand, you break the chain of the human bond. If you break the link, you diminish our strength as a people. I firmly believe that we are as strong as our weakest counterparts. When we fail to offer a helping hand, turn a blind eye to the needs of others or ignore the cries of those who suffer, we become disconnected. It's a disconnect that undermines our resilience. It's a disconnect that limits your access to others on an emotional and spiritual level. For instance, if you can't meet people where they are and be genuinely invested in their well-being, especially those who don't look, act or think like you, you run the risk of not having the foundation necessary to build culturally diverse relationships, sustainable communities and ultimately a better world.

You Don't Need a Lot to Make a Difference

The truth of the matter is, it only takes a little to make a world of difference. Sometimes, telling a story can give someone all they need to perk up and show up in the world. Your story can be the catalyst to inspire change by turning breakdowns into breakthroughs, or turning a mess into a message that someone can relate to. As a result, your words can be a gift that keep on giving especially when the listener can't trust their own story to transform their negative thoughts. Your story then becomes the mental and inspirational anthem that uplifts and empowers them to take action.

However, for those who have the means of making monetary contributions, they are able to make a bigger impact. It's for this reason I often find myself demanding what it is I deserve as a business owner so that I can give back in a way that allows me to become more influential among those I serve. This idea comes as a result of me wanting the financial means necessary to influence others in a way that allows them to be and do better.

As a business owner, I am passionate and committed to helping others cultivate a winning performance by empowering them to find their voice. I realize that in order for me to serve my tribe and expand my reach, I must stand firm in my "ask" and be genuinely unapologetic about it. How can I neglect or dishonor my human potential and value yet want to give back to others at my highest level? I can't... it's impossible. This means that I can't give something that I am not willing to ask for and if I don't get it by way of my products and services, I will limit my ability to maximize my performance by giving a fraction of what's possible. Therefore, I would say this to the person who is selling themselves short yet seeking to do good in the world. I would say, "Make your willingness to help be bigger than your hurt." Why? Because sometimes it can be uncomfortable, even painful, asking for the things we deserve.

When you allow other people's needs to be bigger than your fears, your ability to give is that much more impactful. One, you take the pressure off of you and are able to focus on what truly matters. As a result, you rob your fears of their power over your generous spirit. Two, you will find yourself engaging in what's known as the law of reciprocity. Which simply means, when you do something for someone else, they are likely to turn around and do something for you which allows it to be mutually beneficial. Imagine a world where everyone applied the law of reciprocity, then imagine how drastically our world would change on a fundamental level. At the very least, I believe the following questions will give you a better idea of how your ability to give or not to give will serve you and others.

- Do you consider volunteering to be one of your values? Why or why not?

- What can you offer someone that has the potential to change their lives?

- When was the last time you volunteered to help someone who has helped you and how do you think it made them feel?

It's Better to Be a Helper Than a Hero

When giving back to others, it's better to have the mindset of a helper rather than a hero. When you aim to help, it becomes more beneficial to you and the recipient. For instance, when you are not the "hero," that person who feels the need to save the day, you don't feel the added pressure to make a difference. You don't feel as if someone's life is totally dependent on the choices you do or don't make. You're less likely to feel as though there is a fire ablaze and you're the only one who can safely put it out. Why? Because you understand your role and the limitations of it. You understand that there are days when you feel as though you have these metaphorical holes in your cape. Although you want to rise and shine, you can only do so much and only go so far.

> When you allow other people's needs to be bigger than your fears, your ability to give is that much more impactful.

When you act as the helper, you realize that there is a power greater than yourself at work. You realize the act of giving is greater than you, which means you keep your giving in perspective. You know that you are making a difference, you know that what you do matters, however you also know that your act of kindness is derived from your humanity and not from any heroic qualities. Qualities that cause you to appear extraordinary or where you give the perception that you have super powers and you can do it all.

As much as we would like to do it all, the reality is we can't. We have to choose our battles. We have to give of ourselves, our gifts and talents with humility and compassion. We can't be afraid to show our vulnerability. We must let people know that we may not have all the answers or resources but we can do what we can when we can. Super heroes do exist, but only on TV.

One of the best things about being seen as a helper rather than a hero is that people will naturally view you as hero. It will have nothing to do with a bigger-than-life ego or a relentless drive to save the world. By simply helping and doing it from a place of generosity, empathy and love, people will believe that you are bigger than life. In their world, you are their healer, rescuer, guiding light, salvation, strength and/or calm in the midst of their storm. So you see, helping others doesn't mean that you have to have a mindset of being bigger than life. It simply means humbling yourself enough, sometimes in the most fundamental ways. to change a life.

If you can make the time, trust me, it's worth it. Maybe volunteering at a hospital or getting baptized at church isn't for you. That's okay, because as long as there are children, we will need mentors to cultivate and nourish their precious minds. As long as there are elderly they will need a helping hand. As long as people continue to self- destruct through drugs and alcohol, they will need builders in their lives to reconstruct their self-esteem, strengthen their spiritual foundation, and help tear down the walls of emotional pain. It starts with people like you and me. You can make a difference. It starts with you not relying on your super hero cape to allow you to fly high and change the world, but rather your innate capabilities to change a life. Remember, you don't have to act like a hero. It's a good chance in someone's eyes, you already are a hero.

Time to Rise and Shine!

- *Find Ways to Empower Others*

  Give someone the inspiration to see, act, or feel differently about themselves. I believe one of the greatest gifts you can give someone is the opportunity for them to acknowledge their strengths and assets so that they can come to appreciate who they are and what they offer the world. Unfortunately, some people opt out of this opportunity because they may feel as though the task outweighs their level of confidence or because they don't have what it takes.

  Sometimes it can be something as simple as giving someone a smile or complimenting them on something that is often overlooked or taken for granted. Or, maybe they simply want someone to listen to what they have been through or are currently going through. Become a good listener for those who may feel as if they are never heard. Sometimes it's not always money that's needed the most. There are cases when just making the time to be a good listener is enough.

  Regardless of who you are, I believe it's safe to say that we all want to be heard and to have our thoughts and feelings valued. On a fundamental level, people want to feel as if they are appreciated and that their words matter. When we make ourselves accessible to others by simply listening, what we are essentially communicating is "You are worth my time, and what you have to say has value. I could be doing anything at this moment, and I chose to spend it with you. Why? Because you're worth it!"

- ## Make Volunteering Personal
  Volunteer for a specific cause that not only addresses the plight of humanity, but also allows you to rise and shine as your best self. When you choose to give the best of you it will inevitably bring out the best in others. Therefore, identify a cause that resonates with you and gives you a sense of purpose. Allow it to bring forth all the gifts and talents you may possess to inspire those who lack good health, hope and happiness.

  Let your purpose and passion be the driving force to develop the empathy needed to cultivate a human connection. It's then that you will create an optimal experience for yourself and the recipient of your good deeds. For instance, when you bring the best of you to the worst of their circumstances the result is favored towards a more positive and rewarding outcome. It's only when you seek to validate and own your internal resources can you be the best resource for others.

  To tap into your most prized and valuable resources ask yourself the questions that matter most. What are my most valuable assets as a person that could benefit others in the most impactful way? What skills do I possess that I may be underestimating and could use to change someone's life? Who in particular could best benefit from what I have to offer? These questions not only help you to get focused, but they also allow you to become strategic in using your resources in the most responsible and efficient way.

- *Be Intentional When Expressing Gratitude*

  Express gratitude to someone for helping you become the person you are today. In life, it's easy to forget that we didn't become the person we are today as a result of our own merit or ingenuity. We had help along the way. Therefore, be inclined to reach out to those who have reached out to you. Call them unexpectedly to let them know they made a difference. Even better, write them a letter and mail it. A mailed letter will reflect a more caring, thoughtful, and compassionate you.

  As we have progressed to more of a technologically driven society where we have become more reliant on cell phones and the conveniences they offer, the thought of writing a letter to someone seems like time wasted and an outdated approach to communicating. Writing someone a letter hasn't gone out of style and it never will.

  Random acts of kindness are another way of showing gratitude. Look for moments when helping someone is least expected. When you're not looking for a thank you, or any form of recognition when it's all said and done. For instance, pay for someone's meal, particularly the driver behind you after leaving the drive through window. They will appreciate you immensely. I know this, because it happened to me! People come to expect the ordinary. When you do something out of the ordinary, especially when it's for the good of mankind, people take notice. As a result, they become emotionally grateful and delighted by your selfless giving.

Chapter 4

BE FORGIVING; GIVE YOURSELF A SECOND CHANCE

There is a fine balance between honoring the past
and losing yourself in it. For example, you can acknowledge
and learn from mistakes you made, and then move on
and refocus on the now. It is called forgiving yourself.
Eckhart Tolle

Lightning bugs, clotheslines, and southern hospitality are images that can't seem to escape my mind, nor should they. I've come to accept that they are a by-product of my environment. These childhood memories are so ingrained in my psyche that when I hear the words Louisville, Kentucky something comes over me like a bath of warm water. Water that could temporarily soothe even the most depressing and dispirited memories. However, those heartfelt images would only represent a fraction of my experience of living with my grandparents, experiences which made my living there complex and unstable to say the least.

Mornings at my grandparents' house would often begin with a sense of harmony and a feeling of togetherness, causing me to feel protected and out of harm's way. The day would often start with my grandparents rising at the crack of dawn in preparation for work. Grandmamma was a housekeeper at a local hospital and Granddaddy was a construction worker.

Soon after I would awaken, I would often smell the combination of coffee, fried eggs, and a skillet of sausage that would arouse even the most unresponsive sleeper in the house. Once I got a whiff of the aroma, it somehow managed to wake me up before I could hear my grandmother's commanding yet caring voice say, "Michelle, are you up? It's time to get ready for school. Girl, do you hear me?" Little did she know, my appetite and the food she was preparing already had a morning date, and I was willing, ready, and able to make it down those narrow and creaky stairs.

Grandmamma was really good at multitasking. Between getting dressed, preparing breakfast, making sure I was up and had lunch money for school, she always seemed to be on her game. I would often catch her putting on her makeup in our cramped and outdated bathroom to complement the baby blue uniform she wore to work while singing a gospel hymn.

She had a uniform that was subtly stained in various places yet showed its wear more prominently around her stomach area perhaps due to her full figure, but her warm smile and motherly demeanor managed to somehow pose as a distraction. However, it was the look in her eyes that revealed her story. If you looked long and hard enough you could see the depths of her pain and the discomfort of her restless soul.

Although I was a teenager in high school, I was old enough to know that if I were to entertain my curiosity by trying to understand her hidden truths, it would have been too much too bear. However, I could only imagine what it was like to have a husband who at times seemed to engage in excessive bouts of drinking. She also had children who unfortunately found themselves fighting the same battles.

So rather than go to that dark and uncomfortable place, I tried to stay in the moment and focus on the life that was unfolding in front of my very eyes.

I would notice the skillet sizzling from the high heat on the stove while Granddaddy sat at the kitchen table drinking a cup of coffee and reading the newspaper. At times, it seemed as if the noise that resulted from our morning routine was nothing less than an improvised symphony that produced organic and rhythmic sounds. Sounds that were created by way of the turning of Grandaddy's newspaper. It often resembled the unwrapping of Christmas gifts on a cold winter day. Then there was the thunderous crackling of sausage that brought excitement like the fireworks on the Fourth of July. They could definitely make your soul sing, especially on an empty stomach. Then there were footsteps that created melodic yet random thumps, reminding me of one of the opening scenes in the movie *Annie*. Except the way we expressed our hard knock life was through our unconscious actions and pain-ridden silence.

Grandaddy's contribution to the mornings was often a cucumber salad that he seemed to take great pride in. It rested at the center of the table as if it were on display to be adorned. It was a subtle addition, especially coming from a man who could cook a pot of chitterlings with a swiftness, but it had its place, and I loved it. Unfortunately, these feelings of harmony and togetherness could prove to be short-lived by the end of the day.

My grandmother's multitasking seemed to be unraveling at the seams, particularly during my high school years. The arguing, fussing, and fighting was a continuous battle and my uncle Ronnie managed on many occasions to be the impetus. It was obvious that his values and the way in which he demonstrated them was in conflict with showing respect for others within our household. His selfish and unruly nature knew no boundaries and as a result compromised his relationships and his ability to develop a sense of compassion for others. What did that mean for me? It meant compromising my integrity because I was often asked to give up and give in to his behavior, which was rude and offensive.

If I was sitting in "his seat" when it was time to watch "his show" I was forced to move. If I spoke my mind in self-defense I was cursed at or told to shut my mouth. This would prove to only be the tipping point to the mental distress I was exposed to. The many nights that resulted in his tyrannical behavior because he couldn't get what he wanted when he wanted it would disrupt the household to the degree of needing to call the police. Consequently, with broken furniture, emotional distress, and mental fatigue I was beginning to feel as though I had had enough. His behavior was not only taking a toll on my grandparents, but it also caused me to feel a sense of shame amongst my peers in my neighborhood.

There were times when my grandmother would ask, "Chelle, when you graduate from school and find yourself a job, are you going to come home and cook and take care of your grandmamma and granddaddy?" I, without question, would respond by saying, "Yes Grandmamma, of course I will." My response seemed to provide the reassurance she needed to feel valued and appreciated. It was as if I had given her a Band-Aid for a wounded heart that couldn't seem to heal otherwise. As if my words gave her a sense of inner peace, where she could sit back and relax and anticipate the day her and my grandfather could home to a hot and soulful meal made with lots of love. Unfortunately, I was not able to honor my promise. I could no longer bear the unruly and dysfunctional environment I was exposed to. I knew that once I graduated from high school I needed a change.

I wanted to be exposed to new people, places, and things. So, when my father came to Louisville to attend my high school graduation, I unloaded a question that would literally send him running off of my grandmother's front porch. "Daddy, I want to come back to Minnesota to live with you." As he ran off the front porch to his car, I stood there speechless. I was confused and there was no one there to help me understand his reaction, but it really didn't matter. In spite of our history together, I felt as if I didn't have much to lose, and besides, I felt as if I was old enough to protect myself from any harm my father could potentially cause.

I ignored his rejection. I proceeded with my exit strategy as if he invited me to come back with him with open arms. I think I get my stubbornness from my father, so if anyone is to blame, well, there you go. I say this with humor and a light heart because truly the reason I was prepared to leave was so much bigger than he and I. It was about giving myself another chance and investing in my future. It was about establishing a form of financial stability to one day create a better life for my family. Fortunately, my father soon agreed to take me back with him. I later suspected that his silence was driven by his lifestyle of being single and he wasn't prepared for any additional responsibility. I guess you can say it was bittersweet.

For some time, I found it hard to forgive myself for leaving Louisville once again. As the oldest of four children, I felt a sense of responsibility, a responsibility I cherished as a teenager, but found it difficult to uphold. In addition, I felt as if my grandparents had been counting on me and had invested their time to ensure that they contributed to my upbringing as best as they could. My grandmother especially encouraged me to stay in church and always show gratitude towards those who lent a helping hand. Unfortunately, I felt as if I didn't give them a proper return on their investment. I felt as if they deserved so much more than a long distance phone call or a yearly visit. My grandparents were counting on me to be there and just like a thief in the night, I was gone. Unfortunately, there was a price to pay for my decision.

Often, I would come home to visit only to be scrutinized and ridiculed by specific family members. I distinctly remember being told that I looked like I had two black eyes as I sat on my grandmother's front porch shortly after arriving for a visit. I so desperately wanted to be welcomed with open arms, but apparently that wasn't so. It would be sarcastic remarks relating to the way I talked. I was told that I talked as if I was "white." After hearing it a number of times, I came to the conclusion that her intentions were not meant as a joke, as her insensitive and punitive words stung like a bee. However, just like a bee sting, it hurts at first, but with time you manage to bear the pain. Over the years, I've come to accept who I am and the decisions I've made in my life. Actually, it's because of my decisions that I have been able to withstand some of the turbulent storms in my life, but also have a greater appreciation for the times I didn't.

As I look back on the years that my grandparents helped me to become the person I am today, I would like to think that although I wasn't there to take care of them in their time of need, I hope they found solace in knowing that they instilled in me the values and wisdom needed for me to take care of myself. So you see, I no longer blame myself for putting my needs first. I have forgiven myself and because I have, I don't feel the weight of the world on my shoulders. I don't let other people's personal agendas, unwarranted remarks or distorted views interfere with my growth. I have made an intentional effort to rise above limiting words and actions created by those who appear not to serve my best interest. I share this with you because I want you to have a forgiving heart not just with others, but even more so, with yourself.

Practice Self-Compassion with a Growth Mindset

Your ability to forgive your past mistakes highly influences your ability to rise up and perform favorably in the pursuit of your goals. Forgiving yourself allows you to embrace your mistakes and perceived failures while minimizing the resentment and bitterness aimed at yourself with self-compassion. It allows you to create emotional space for a healthier well-being while minimizing emotional toxicity so you can expand and grow in other areas of your life.

Self-compassion is a way of providing what I call Inner Body Insurance. This means whenever your actions are out of alignment with your expectations and values, rather than feel depressed or shameful, you access the power within you: that reservoir of inner strength to forgive yourself by accepting what has happened and not holding yourself hostage as a result of it. Keep in mind accepting doesn't mean that you are in compliance with your wrongdoings. It doesn't mean that you don't feel remorse or regret for what you have done, but it does mean that you understand the scope and reality of what you have done.

Rick Hanson, author of *Resilient*, says, "Acceptance can sit alongside other reactions. For example, a person can be outraged by an injustice and accept that it's a reality. Accepting doesn't mean complacency or giving up. We can accept something while at the same time trying to make it better." Unfortunately, there are underlying problems which prevent us from accepting our reality and attaining Inner Body Insurance. For instance, it could simply be we don't understand the importance of acceptance. When we accept ourselves for who we are and what we've done we optimize our resilience in various ways.

Self-Acceptance is Knowing the Difference Between Shame and Guilt

When we accept ourselves, we in turn are more accepting of others. We strengthen our self-efficacy because we believe we have control over the challenges life brings. We are able to befriend ourselves in the most intimate way. Another underlying issue of attaining Inner Body Insurance is that we confuse shame with guilt. Although they may appear to have similarities, they are in fact different. Shame has the tendency to have a negative connotation while guilt is seen as less detrimental to your overall health and well-being. Brene Brown, author of *The Gifts of Imperfection*, says, "Shame is about who we are, and guilt is about our behaviors. Guilt is just as powerful as shame, but its effect is often positive while shame often is destructive." Understanding that makes a world of difference as it relates to your development. When you feel empowered to change your behavior you gain more control over the outcome of your circumstances. You don't allow yourself to identify with your problems. They don't become part of you. They are more likely to be associated with what you do rather than who you are. However, it all starts in the mind. If you can change your mind you can change your behavior and if you can change your behavior you have the power to change your life.

What experiences or thoughts are you holding yourself accountable for that are slowing down the progression of your success? What are you holding on to that is tainting your ability to attract and or manifest new opportunities into your life? Whatever it is, it must be recognized and addressed to optimize your performance and lead a life of resilience.

Whatever is Keeping You in the Dark Must Be Brought to Light

You cannot rise and shine and deliver your best performance if you continue to punish yourself based on past mistakes. These are mistakes which you have absolutely no control over in the sense that they happened in the past. We continue to invest in them mentally and emotionally because we either set unrealistic expectations, compare ourselves with others, feel as though we are not deserving, or strive to be perfect, which, as we know, is an illusion. The moment we suspend judgement on who we are as a person so that we can transcend into our higher self is the moment our perceived wrongdoings will manifest with clarity, allowing us to make a more accurate assessment of the situation.

It's clarity that will allow you to stop presenting yourself as a human punching bag. However, to be clear, I am not suggesting that it is abnormal or out of character to get down on yourself during moments of defeat. I believe it's safe to say that at various points in our lives, we feel as if we have lost a battle and, may I add, some a lot more than others, yet I don't believe we would be human if we expected otherwise. On the other hand, when we find ourselves in self-defeating situations and we allow them to define our character rather than the situation at hand, our ability to "bounce back" is significantly reduced. This may lead to lower self-esteem, a negative self-image and a higher probability of experiencing self-victimization. Once again, I am also not suggesting that forgiving ourselves comes with ease or a lack of upheaval.

Courage is Necessary to Cultivate Resilience

Forgiveness by way of self-compassion requires an abundance of courage. It requires you to surrender unfounded judgements and move beyond self-accusations to a place where you can cultivate a healthy well-being. A well-being that is formed through self-love, compassion, and personal acceptance to live freely and without regret. This is what I want for you. I want you to get to a place where you can abandon any shame you have experienced so you don't stunt your personal growth any longer. This will allow you to rise to the occasion by embracing new opportunities and attracting new things into your life.

Oprah Winfrey once said, "The great courageous act that we must all do, is to have the courage to step out of our history and past so that we can live our dreams." You see, when you step out of your history and past you leave behind the parts of you that have a tendency to exacerbate your failures and imperfections. It's the parts of you that hold your ambitions captive because you can't see or experience the truth of what is, but rather you have become a victim to what was. Why? Because you have chosen to base your identity and self-worth on past experiences. Experiences that have distorted your reality of who you really are and of what you are really capable of. What we all must be reminded of is that the gift of life and the gift of attaining our wildest dreams can only be realized by courageously embracing the moment. You can start your journey to living courageously to attain your hopes and dreams by answering the following questions.

- What dreams have you put on hold as a result of blaming yourself for past mistakes?
- What events in your life have robbed you of self-compassion and caused you to lose sleep?

- What situations have deterred you from participating in new ventures that have kept well intentioned people out of your life? These are people who could have helped you accomplish your dreams and goals.

These are questions that are worthy of thought and exploration. It's in these answers and your ability to enhance your self-awareness that you will begin to see the truth behind your misguided judgements. Keep in mind that you don't have to forgive yourself of something enormous or catastrophic to act on it and reap its rewards. When you learn to forgive yourself for things which may appear trivial, it lays the groundwork for you to implement new skills during life-altering situations. It requires the same mind and skill-set to battle what potentially could be your performance of a lifetime.

Be brave and see what's on the other side of forgiveness. I assure you, the other side is filled with endless possibilities. Why? Because the definition of who you are becomes broader and more refined as you seek the truth by filtering the impurities of your experiences with an open mind. As a result, it allows you to view yourself as someone worthy of redemption. Your performance, whether perceived good or bad, has relevance and substance that should be embraced. Don't let it stop you from developing the emotional maturity needed to think and live beyond your limiting beliefs. Speak your truth not only to others, but more importantly to yourself. Try it…your ability to rise and shine depends on it.

> When you learn to forgive yourself for things which may appear trivial, it lays the groundwork for you to implement new skills during life-altering situations.

Time to Rise and Shine!

• *Accept That You Are Human*

When you embrace the humanity in you it is much easier to embrace your imperfections and wrongdoings. You come to an understanding that your shortcomings and the things that you have done that negatively reflect on your character do not have to define who you are as a person. You are human. Humans make mistakes. Therefore, acknowledge them and take the higher road. Forgive yourself so that you can reduce mental stress, get emotionally unstuck and contribute to your overall health and well-being.

Accepting you are human requires you to be brutally honest with yourself by looking at your life through a window rather than a tunnel. A window's view will give you greater clarity and allow you to see a bigger, more realistic version of your life. As a result, you not only see your regrettable mistakes, but also your well-deserved accomplishments. You are not looking at your life from a one-sided perspective, which is essential to embracing your humanity. Ask yourself, what is it costing me to not forgive myself and is it worth it? Why do I choose to hold on to something that continues to hinder my spiritual and intellectual growth? Why do I not hold my self-worth in high enough regard to cultivate self-compassion? It's when you can answer these questions truthfully that you will begin to shed the painful emotions of shame and guilt.

• *Let Your Mistakes Make You, Not Break You*

Try to avoid giving your mistakes too much of your personal power. When you give power to those things that create barriers in your life, you become limited in your ability to live a healthy and satisfying life. You will find that you are compromising your potential to be the best you can be. Therefore, rather than harbor debilitating emotions or feelings of angst that could rob you of your resilience, learn to capitalize on the experience so that it will make you into a better person rather than break you into pieces.

Let your mistakes boost your resilience by first owning them. Ownership of your mistakes communicates to yourself and others that you understand the importance of being responsible for your life. It demonstrates you are adept in the skills of accountability and self-regulation. Secondly, uncover the meaning in your mistakes by understanding the core emotions they evoke and why. When you understand the emotions and the values they are connected to, you begin to understand and have a greater appreciation for your perceived wrongdoings. Thirdly, look for solutions and not safety. Make decisions and identify actions that will better serve you the next time around. If they cause a sense of joy and inner peace or they result in you becoming a better human being, then you know you are on the right track. On the other hand, if you choose safety over finding solutions you're more likely to avoid the need to actively manage your feelings or the circumstance at hand. This approach can unfortunately perpetuate self-hate and shaming. Why? It becomes much easier to blame yourself than to change yourself.

- *Live In The Moment Not The Past*
  If you make a conscious decision to live in the moment as much as possible, you will have less time to dwell on the past and speculate about the future. You will have more time to engage in solution-oriented thinking allowing you to transcend beyond your mistakes to rid yourself of emotional turmoil. Therefore,

your energy and focus will not be spent on what you did wrong or consumed by what you could have done differently. It will be spent on creating a new narrative that will support you on your journey to letting go and pressing forward in the present moment.

To live in the moment, you want to be intentional about your thoughts. For instance, when your thoughts have you stuck in the past, immediately connect to your higher self by grounding yourself in the moment. As your self-limiting narrative begins to unfold in your mind, take an active approach by redirecting your thoughts with positive affirmations. Affirmations are things we say to ourselves to affirm our thoughts and alter our identity. They are powerful statements that get re-enforced in our conscious and subconscious mind to change our thinking patterns.

If you find that you are blaming yourself for past mistakes, rather than say, "I am such an idiot. What was I thinking?" Instead say, "I own my mistakes. I am not perfect, but I am present." Or, "I wish I could go back in time and do things differently." Instead, you could say, "I can't change my past, but as long as I am living, I have the power to change my future." Remember, your past may have shaped you, but it doesn't have to define you.

Chapter 5

RISE WITH THE POWER OF RESILIENCE

When it comes to our collective health,
how we deal with the multiple crises and problems around us
also depends on the power of context
—in other words, our resilience.
Arianna Huffington

When applying to be a student at the University of Minnesota, I knew that it would be a battle. I knew my grades were lacking in merit and promise. I was also cognizant of the fact that I would pay the price for my lack of attentiveness and disengaged behavior in high school. This was primarily due to me not realizing my potential. However, due to my persistent and resilient nature, I decided to shamelessly pursue my academic goal, which was to become a psychologist.

Being that my grades were not up to par with my ambitions, I was subtly dissuaded and encouraged to choose another career path. I am proud to say that my hard work paid off. Although, I didn't pursue psychology, I was later accepted to the School of Human Ecology where I had an opportunity to earn a master's degree in education. I was beyond excited, yet I knew it was essential that I maintain my grades and meet the academic requirements necessary to attain my degree.

My accelerated master's program proved to be very demanding. Finding time to eat in between classes, was more like an arduous task than a necessity. Did I mention finding the time to study? Studying was a rather new concept in my vernacular and daily tasks. Self-doubt and low academic expectations prior to this point had become part of my identity, like the coarse and kinky hair that sprouted from the roots of my head.

At times, when my self-esteem felt compromised, like I was an imposter, I found myself wondering if I was worthy of being accepted to such an esteemed program. "How did I get here? Can I meet the expectations of my professors, or will I become another statistic? Who am I to have such high hopes and dreams?" These were all self-defeating thoughts that had begun to consume my mind. However, through hard work and a strong support system, I managed to find the internal strength and mental fortitude to rise and shine. Things were looking good and nothing was going to stop me from achieving my goals. Little did I know I would soon be reminded of this thing called life and the impact it could have on one's hopes and dreams.

It's November 3, 2000. At approximately 5:00am my phone began to ring. I awakened startled and confused, wondering who could be calling at such an hour. Although my head couldn't make sense of the persistent and intrusive sound, in my heart I knew it would be a message that would ultimately change my life. Unfortunately, I was right. It was my cousin Amanda on the other end of the phone. Her dull and lifeless voice slowly began to convey a heavy and dreadful message. "Michelle, Grandmamma, just shot Granddaddy. We think that she was trying to shoot Ronnie, but accidently shot Granddaddy."

I felt as if I had been punched in the stomach repeatedly, my breath taken away with each excruciating blow. I felt as if I was in the dark literally and figuratively as I stood in my bedroom at a loss for words. Within seconds, the shock that initially silenced my pain was forcefully expelled from my limp and deflated body. As my legs regained their strength, I began to scream and run uncontrollably through our two bedroom apartment. I couldn't make sense of what I had just heard and no matter how much my husband tried to comfort and console me it was never enough.

Why would she try to kill my Uncle Ronnie? She was the one who protected him at all costs. She was the one who compromised her marriage at the expense of his ill-mannered and often shameless ways. What changed? Had he finally crossed a line to a point of no return? Had she come to embrace her self-worth and was willing to protect it to the point of taking his life? If so, why now? It wouldn't be long before a more accurate account of this tragic moment in our family's lives would be revealed.

According to my cousin Brenda, who was at my grandparent's house at the time of the shooting, my grandparents were in a heated argument that lasted well into the early morning hours. The argument apparently had something to do with giving my Uncle Ronnie a birthday party. After some time, my grandmother removed herself from the bedroom where the heated exchange had initially taken place. At that moment she seemed to find refuge in one of the living room chairs. I would imagine it was near the living room window where she often sat after a long days work to rest her feet and ease her mind. Unfortunately, her goal in seeking peace in her home would be short-lived. Soon after, my grandfather came from the bedroom and was now arguing with Ronnie. The situation seemed to escalate especially after my grandmother was once again entangled in the argument. It was apparent that my grandfather had reached a boiling point to the point where he threw liquid Drano on her. Sensing that she needed to protect herself and that her life was in danger, she went to the bedroom, found her gun and then shot him multiple times. She never served time in jail, but she was placed on home incarceration.

As I tried to wrestle with his death and the heart-wrenching actions that led up to it, to manage the pain, I desperately tried to find the shine in my whine. I thought about the many times he had shown me love. As a child, sugar was one of my first loves. There wasn't anything that made me happier than going across the street to the candy store, also known as Mr. Steven's, to purchase my favorite treats. Krispy Kreme doughnuts, Now and Laters, and Zero candy bars ranked high on my list. However, first I needed the money to indulge in my sweet pleasures. Granddaddy always seemed to be the key to my salvation. "Granddaddy, can I have some money to go to the candy store?" With eyes on the verge of conjuring up tears, a voice that had a pitch that seem to rise with the progression of each word from my mouth, and a face that resembled the look of an old miserable woman rather than a spirited and cheerful child seemed to be the right combination to touch his heart.

In spite of him appearing tired after a long day of work, he always managed to find it within himself to give whether he could afford to or not. I could tell that the outcome would be in my favor when he would walk from the kitchen to his bedroom. He would then lift up the white doily that served as a placemat for the cable box and underneath it is where he kept his loose change. Once his big and powerful hands released those coins in the palms of my dainty outstretched hands, I was beyond grateful. However, it was the words that followed that mattered the most. "Michelle you watch out for those cars, you hear me? And make sure you look both ways!" The tone of his voice soothed my soul in a way that forcefully yet lovingly captured my attention.

The interesting part was his eyes looking directly into mine said more than his words ever could. The look in his eyes seemed to tell a story that wasn't often told yet rested in the depths of his mind and soul. At that moment, I resurrected those distant thoughts and pensive feelings. The intensity of his eyes and the seriousness of his face revealed that those words weren't just about me, but about a previous loss, unresolved pain, or unhealed wounds. I could feel the energy was different. I could feel as though he had something to lose that was worth significantly more than the loose change he had just placed in my hand moments before. It was abundantly clear he didn't want to lose me.

I was once told that the reason why my grandfather never drove a car was because he was in a really bad car accident. Everyone in the car died, except him. I've asked various family members to confirm what I had heard, but to my surprise, no one could. I would like to believe this was an untold story between me and my grandfather. A story that he entrusted me with that would further seal our bond. Or, it could have just been an unfounded rumor to dramatize his reasons for not driving. Either way, whether this is true or not, I knew that my grandfather was emotionally invested in my survival. He wanted to keep me safe and out of harm's way and that is all that mattered. What I did find to be true was that my grandfather was called Shoeman among his peers. They called him Shoeman because he had a tendency to walk everywhere he went. Maybe this would explain why he was so protective of me crossing the street. Maybe he was keenly aware of what could transpire on those streets which he did not want me to fall victim to. My grandfather was a complex man. Yes, he could be abrasive and have a hypercritical temperament at times. I would suspect this was partly attributed to his use of alcohol, but he was also human. He was also a man with adult children in the home who didn't seem to respect his manhood let alone fatherhood; just as my grandmother tolerated a lot, so did he.

No, we can't bring him back, but the memories we shared, and the moments we had, will live in my heart forever. The fact that my grandmother started to experience dementia before she died and couldn't remember how my grandfather passed away was disheartening. "Chelle what happened to Granddaddy?" Like my grandfather's eyes, hers was filled with loss, unresolved pain, and told a story of unhealed wounds, except in her case, she didn't know why.

Developing the courage to share this news with my advisor at the University of Minnesota was incredibly difficult and overwhelming. I remember being asked if I wanted to drop out and start the program over again at a later time. Sure, that would be the most obvious and logical choice, however, it wasn't an easy one. I had worked so hard up to that point. I was in an accelerated master's program and my schedule could be grueling at times. After many hours of soul searching and reflecting on my life, I knew that my grandfather would not have wanted me to quit. He would want me to continue on my journey towards becoming all that I could be. How could I let him down? How could I say no, when he and God already told me yes? The more I thought about it, the more it became clear that I didn't have a choice. The thought of finishing what I started was no longer an option, but rather a personal mission.

Needless to say, I stayed in the program, but that decision didn't come without a cost. It was a constant battle. Emotionally, I struggled every day at the thought of having lost my grandfather, and not knowing the outcome of my grandmother's future, as well as my own. Regardless of the circumstances, I knew I had to rise up, but even more than I had ever done before. I knew that continuing on this path might require more out of me than I had to give at the time. Once I came to the conclusion that the rewards were greater than the cost, the rest was history. Not only did I graduate with my master's degree, I was also recognized for my academic achievements. I rose up in a big way. I was living a dream. A dream I thought would never come to fruition. The day I walked down the aisle after receiving my degree, I remember looking at my family and thinking, "I did it!"

The most inspiring part of my story isn't the fact that I graduated, but rather that I was able to rise in the face of adversity in spite of the odds. Odds that could have brought me to my knees and robbed me of the possibility of ever rising up to realize my potential. The possibility of me not stepping up to muster the strength to stand in my power with self-confidence, determination, and forgiveness. It was the accumulation of these qualities along with the unending support of my family and the staff at the University of Minnesota that helped me to attain the resilience needed to rise up and show up. It's because of who I chose to be at that time and the person they aspired for me to be that I was able to refrain from taking the path of least resistance.

Accept Who You Are to Become All That You Can Be

There is no secret to rising and shining. No one has been granted special privileges that afford them the opportunity to overcome challenges, make sound and just decisions, and navigate through some of the most difficult and life-changing moments. However, those who do succeed and appear to have mastered the art of rebounding from their problems tend to take on the characteristics of individuals who possess the qualities of resilience.

Resilience is simply the ability to overcome adversity by thinking and acting in a way that cultivates a life of sustainability for optimal health and well-being. It provides the motivation necessary to disregard self-limiting thoughts and face insurmountable barriers in the pursuit of your goals.

Resilience is what gives you the fortitude to rise beyond your fears and search for meaning in everything that is and was. It's what helps to revive your spirit when it has been broken and bruised. It's what transforms you into the person you aspire to be rather than keeping you stuck in the status quo causing you to always wonder who you could be.

Without resilience there would be no opportunities to conquer victorious feats and rejoice in moments of achievement. As a result you would compromise the spark of hope that is needed for you to shine and live your best life. Why? Because when you compromise the light from within, the light that is responsible for making you whole, there will always be a fraction of you that will remain in the dark.

We as a people aspire to be resilient by nature. We want to be rescued from the trials and tribulations of life by acting on our inner power to deliver our best performance. We perform best when our sanity is restored and we have control over our thoughts and actions, which can lead us astray if we are not grounded in our values. It's for this reason why developing the skills to be resilient is essential to our personal growth. Resilience allows us to overcome life experiences that have robbed us of our joy and humanity.

It's what helps us to function and combat our day-to-day adversities that if not handled properly could lead to chronic stress and other physical ailments. According to *Harvard Health Publishing*, "Stress increases blood sugar and can make diabetes worse. It can create high blood pressure and cause insomnia. Chronic stress also increases the risk of heart disease, heartburn, and many other health problems." On the other hand, resilience empowers you to fight for your dreams by not surrendering to your fears. When your fears begin to outweigh your passion you are in jeopardy of losing hope. You increase the chances of your mind focusing on things that do not serve you. If it doesn't serve you, then it has the potential to harm you.

Resilience Requires You to Be Resourceful

Those who choose to be resilient are resourceful. They look within and beyond themselves to find the right solution to their problems.

They don't pigeonhole themselves by minimizing their paths to attain success. This is achieved by thinking outside the box and becoming self-aware. If you can't see an opportunity you will never be in a position to seize an opportunity to make the best of a situation, but most importantly to become the best of you.

You may be thinking, "What types of resources or opportunities should I be looking for? Or, what resources could I possibly have that are within my power to change the trajectory of my life?" According to Karen Reivich and Andrew Shatte, the authors of *The Resilience Factor*, resilience is comprised of seven qualities. These qualities are what give you the foundation needed to withstand the storms of life. For instance, emotion regulation is the ability to manage your emotions, actions and level of attentiveness by not letting your emotions get the best of you when the world tries to bring out the worst in you.

Impulse control is the ability to forgo instant gratification by having the willpower to act on impulses beyond the present moment. Optimism is feeling hopeful about the future by believing there will be better days. In spite of your unfortunate circumstances, pain and problems, optimistic people believe that there is a light at the end of the tunnel.

Empathy allows you to see life through the other person's eyes to get a sense of what it's like to walk in their shoes. It allows you to get in touch with your humanity so that you can embrace the humanity in others. Causal analysis relates to flexibility and open-mindedness. You're able to look at various solutions to a problem, but more importantly identify a solution that best aligns with the problem.

Self-efficacy is recognizing your capabilities and trusting in them wholeheartedly. You allow yourself to step out on faith by believing in yourself. It's not that you don't acknowledge your limitations, but rather you persist in spite of them. Finally, reaching out is accepting that there is something or someone greater than yourself and outside of yourself to help you bounce back in the face of adversity. It's connecting to resources that extend beyond you to restore your quality of life, to optimize your resilience and to draw strength from others when you would have otherwise given up. However, just to be clear, giving up is not always a sign of failure and defeat, which is why it's important to redefine giving up in the context of your personal circumstances. Needless to say, it can work for you or against you.

For many, giving up is not an option. They fight to keep their passions alive and pursue their purpose sometimes to a fault. They see no justification for embracing alternative paths to attaining their goals. In the meantime, time passes and much is left to be desired, notably unfulfilled hopes and dreams. On the other hand, bouncing back from adversity doesn't necessarily mean you should strive to return to where you started. After failed attempts, if you allow yourself to learn from your mistakes you will find that you are in a better position to know better and do better. Luckily, your starting place isn't from where you left off. More often than not, you're likely to be miles ahead because the experience has shown you and exposed you to new ways of thinking.

Resilience Requires You to Be Flexible

Rather than seeing failure as giving up, see it as an opportunity to rise up after you have been knocked down and beat down in the boxing ring of life. Sometimes where and who you aspire to be is not always who and where you are meant to be. Therefore, your aspirations should not be set in stone. They should be as fluid as the waves in the ocean. They should periodically be reevaluated for their worth as it relates to your vision, passion, and personal aspirations. However, you will want to consider and address various questions when deciding if you should give up or rise up.

It would be remiss of me if I didn't address a caveat that was essential to making this determination. Let's face it, making the decision to pursue your hearts' desires or choosing to let them die is not easy to live with. This is why it's important to do a reality check by asking yourself key questions to keeping you on the right path. The questions below that will widen your perspective and highlight the areas that will strengthen your resilience and self-assuredness.

- Is my pain and suffering outweighing my passion and my desire to act on my purpose and if so, is it worth the fight?

- Am I pursing my goals for myself or am I pursuing my goals to satisfy the wants and needs of others?

- Has my vision changed or does it still reflect my values and aspirations in a way that makes my heart smile and soul sing?

Only you can answer these questions to build and sustain your resilience. Only you have the power to soul search and find meaning in your life. There is no right or wrong answer. It's simply making informed decisions between choosing the right path and being intuitive and flexible enough to let the right path choose you. I firmly believe that when you let the right path choose you, it will allow you to rise and shine and deliver your best performance. It will support you and facilitate a more peaceful and emotionally satisfying journey to becoming the resilient you. Therefore, whatever path you choose, whether it's to rise up or give up, make sure you have done your due diligence to ensure that your decision is justified and clarified.

If you are one of those people who choose to fight and go the distance, this is what I say to you from the depths of my heart: You have made a brave decision. A decision that will at times cause you to experience heartbreak, regrets and feelings of hopelessness to the point where you will want to turn back and give up. In those moments know that the power of hope resides within you. Know that as you sit in the abyss and depths of your sorrows and fight for a glimmer of hope amongst your darkest days, know that the restoration of hope may appear above and beyond your reach. The good news is you don't need arms to reach for many of the things that already reside within you.

Let hope be one of the greatest gifts you give yourself. So that when you are down on your luck, searching for life-changing solutions, or seeking to be rescued from the disappointments of life, you are able to look within to restore it for yourself. Consequently, what you think you can't change will inspire you with hope to create change. It's the hope that once gave your life meaning and made you feel safe and comforted even in the midst of fear and moments of uncertainty. It's what provides the key to your salvation.

Sometimes we may underestimate our ability to generate hope within ourselves simply because we are not taught how powerful we really are. As a result, we go searching for that person or thing that will inspire or motivate us to live our best lives. However, when you are able to see and appreciate the value of your humanity, you simultaneously breed the confidence needed to instill hope, but also rely on it in times of need.

Being Hopeful Helps to Live Your Best Life

Hope is what helps you stay grounded. It's what fuels the inspiration within you to conquer life's battles and persist even when the battle is won. Therefore, keep hope alive. Let it live within you. Let it breathe as if it were a living being. See it for what it is worth and let it inflate your sense of self to show you that hope coupled with faith can be bigger than life itself. So the next time your hope has diminished and evaporated like a puddle of rain on a hot summer day, don't fret, don't cry. Let the hope within rectify your doom and gloom of today so that you can have a brighter future tomorrow. Sometimes, it's a matter of using your imagination to accept the reality of just how bright you are capable of shining.

Imagine you're like a tree nearly broken from your core. The wind done blew you in every direction imaginable, but you held on. The wind done shook all the fruits you had to bear, exposed your vulnerabilities, left you hopeless and in despair, but you held on. Those around you seem to stand tall thriving as they appear to be living their best life. You, on the other hand, are trying to rise up broken and bruised because of all the things in life that have let you down.

What you don't know is there is a source of light in the far distance that shines and is rooting for your rise—the sun. Imagine it wants you to see brighter days. It wants you to get the nourishment you need to be brought back to life to bloom to your potential. What the sun doesn't know is, the light that it shines upon you is a reflection of the light that shines within you. You are the light of the world. Let your light illuminate your dreams. Let it guide you to your purpose so that you live it, and then become it. It's time my friend. It's time to rise and shine!

Hope is what helps you stay grounded.
It's what fuels the inspiration within you to conquer life's battles and persist even when the battle is won.

Time to Rise and Shine

- *Create a Social Network*

  One of the qualities of building resilience is the ability to reach out. Reaching out helps you to connect to external resources that live outside of you and in a sense are bigger than you. They are resources that complement your internal resources by providing you with the extra support needed to foster resilience. One way to accomplish this is to surround yourself with people you know, like and trust. These are individuals you can reach out to when the going gets tough and when you lack the motivation to fight battles that consume you. Give yourself permission to let them help you bear the load. Don't worry about being an inconvenience. If they care about you and your well-being they will understand. They will have an appreciation for your struggles by empathizing with your circumstances.

  Your social network extends beyond those who you may know. It also includes social institutions that are there to assist you in various situations. Whether they are organizations affiliated with religious practices, economic assistance, mental stability, marital, or family support, they all serve as resources to help you develop the resilience needed to overcome obstacles. If you have access to them and they are a solution to your problem, use them. The more support you have to re-establishing stability in your life by overcoming adversity, the sooner you will be in a position to rise and shine.

- *Be Selective in Your Thoughts*

  What you think matters. Your thoughts can either hurt you or help you. However, there is a notable caveat that should be taken into consideration. "Happy" thoughts are not necessarily resilient thoughts. It is for this reason why you want to be aware of your thoughts whether positive or negative. Positive thoughts are more likely to lead to positive actions and outcomes. They are what helps you to maintain the optimism needed to envision a future of endless possibilities. Sometimes, it can be as simple as identifying things that you are grateful for. Things that often go unnoticed, but have value and can bring meaning to your life.

Negative thoughts have the potential to drain you and defeat you. They sabotage your energy and rob you of living in the moment. They have no purpose other than to distract you from the things that truly matter. However, when you are aware of them and are able to manage them you build the resilience needed to rise and shine. If you find that negative thoughts are impeding on your life in a way that hinders your well-being, allow yourself to get present. Once you are present, you are now in a better position to re-frame your thoughts.

- ## Be Optimistic During Times of Defeat
Your ability to be optimistic during times of struggle will often be the difference between sustainable success or perpetual failure. Fortunately, optimism is what helps to keep hope alive. It's what helps you to look forward to brighter days by being open to new possibilities and opportunities. Without optimism there are no seeds of hope to cultivate new beginnings, inspire change or transform lives.

To be optimistic, it's important to differentiate between optimism and Pollyanna optimism. The former is rooted in positivity while the latter is misleading. "Pollyanna optimism" is "When you replace your negative thoughts with an unrealistically optimistic belief." (*The Resilience Factor*, 211). One promising tactic to becoming optimistic is to allow yourself to be inspired by others who are making a big impact in the world. Allow yourself to look for and up to those who use their voice for the greater good of humanity.

For the role model you select, make sure they meet the criteria of resilience. For instance, when they stumbled in trying to make progress, they found a way to get back up to go the distance. When the world stopped providing them the lights to be seen as their best they emerged from the darkness and created their own. Finally, when they were down on their luck they created their own luck through hard work, perseverance and optimism.

Chapter 6

DISCOVER THE FORTUNE IN YOUR FAILURE

I've missed more than 9,000 shots in my career,
I've lost almost 300 games,
26 times I've been trusted to take the game-winning shot...and missed,
I've failed over and over and over again in my life,
and that is why I succeed.
Michael Jordan

After graduating college, I had hopes and dreams of moving to California to pursue an acting career. A career I knew little about, but was willing to take a chance on bringing my childhood dreams to reality. As a child, I would often envision myself acting, whether it was on stage, television, or film. It was as if I was blessed with a calling but didn't have the skill or mind set to receive it or more importantly take the steps to make it a reality.

I remember being asked what I wanted to be when I grew up and when my response was an actress, I was politely yet firmly encouraged to take my life into another direction. "You don't want be an actress; be a nurse." I thought to myself, "Nurse? I have a great deal of appreciation for nurses, but that is not who I aspire to be. First,

I don't like the sight of blood and secondly my heart isn't in it. The thought of being a nurse didn't get me excited or fill my spirit. I wanted to be true to who I was. I wanted to be freed by doing something I loved rather than something I had to do in order to get by.

I sat and watched my grandmother work herself tirelessly over the years. Getting up at 5am to head to work as a housekeeper at a local hospital, while witnessing her nearly break her back to support her family, and also at times, breaking her spirit. Even though she smiled and would be willing to give you all she had, I knew deep down inside she wanted more out of life and if I could have given it to her, I would have. Unfortunately, over the years, my childhood dreams were never nurtured or fully appreciated. Those feelings of excitement would remain dormant inside of me until I was old enough to make my own decisions.

In 1995, I was a contestant in the Ms. Black Minnesota Pageant. During the talent portion of the event, I decided to perform a monologue titled, "I See a Hard Times a Comin." The feeling that came over me as I performed was nothing short of amazing. If that feeling could have been bottled up and sold, I would have been rich for the rest of my life and over the moon with joy.

As I stepped on the stage and took in the audience, I felt a sense of comfort and familiarity. I suspect the familiarity stemmed from the fact that I replayed this image of me performing on stage over and over again in my head, and I loved it. Once I finished, I remember the audience giving me a standing ovation. I became overwhelmed with emotion. The feeling was intoxicating and validating. It helped to further reinforce my purpose and passion for wanting to perform.

In the end, I did not earn the title of Ms. Black Minnesota. However, I did finish as a finalist. On the inside, I felt I was a winner above and beyond the pageant. You see, what happened to me that evening proved that the fire that was burning in me had a place in my life and the hearts of other people. The people in the audience connected with my words; they were inspired by my performance, they cheered with enthusiasm and pride, and because of that, I was a winner. The only difference was, I felt as though I wore my crown on my heart rather than my head. Inspired by this experience, the thought of moving to California was beginning to look more promising. I told my husband that when I graduated with my master's degree that's where I wanted to go and because of his endless support, that's exactly what we did.

The day my husband and I arrived in Los Angeles, I felt a great sense of pride and excitement. "I actually did it!" I thought. I set out to move to Los Angeles and I am finally here. The feeling was new and overwhelming. I didn't know how to contain myself. The first restaurant we ate at was on Venice Beach. When I discovered our waiter was an actor, I nearly lost my mind. My husband, who couldn't help but laugh, reminded me to keep things in perspective and that he would be one of many who I would eventually meet. As I came to my senses, I realized he was probably right.

It wouldn't be long before I learned what it would take to become a successful actress-a lot of hard work. I knew I had to step up if I was going to make it in Hollywood to be recognized as the talented actress I aspired to be. I soon enrolled in the Ruskin School of Acting in Santa Monica. I was determined to hone my craft and become a master of it. I was determined to not let anyone or anything get in my way. Unfortunately, my aspirations would soon be challenged, forcing me to expose my vulnerabilities.

I remember my acting instructor inviting me to take part in a play reading. Not only was I excited to have been selected to participate, but I also knew that it would give me an opportunity to showcase my talents. Yes, we routinely did exercises to further develop our acting skills, but this was different. This opportunity would validate my acting ability. It would demonstrate my understanding of the concept of living truthfully under imaginary circumstances.

It was important for my peers and instructor to see what was special about me: my strengths, capabilities, in bringing my character to life. Although it was a reading, I wanted to leave them wanting more. It was my time and I was ready. As we sat on the floor in a circle, I remember anxiously anticipating my turn to read. However, something started to change and it was not a change I prepared for. The closer it came time for me to speak, the more afraid I became. "What's happening?" I thought. "Why do my mind and body seem to be betraying me? No pun intended, I thought we were on the same page. I thought we were in this together!"

As I started to speak, it became more difficult for me to breathe. Every breath seemed overwhelming and challenging. In hindsight, it seemed easier to breathe during the birth of my two children than reading that play at that moment. I felt as if each breath was draining the life out of me. It was as if I started out as a ripe healthy looking plum that had been diminished to a dried up ole prune who was ready to be eaten alive by my peers. Although, my mouth spoke the words from the script, my mind was screaming the word, "Help!" It didn't appear as if anyone was coming to the rescue any time soon.

I wanted to disappear and forget about my dream. I wanted to smother myself in my grandmother's arms like when she would smother pork chops in gravy. But unless I was a genie in a bottle or possessed special powers, that simply wasn't going to happen. So what did I do? I managed to get through the script one agonizing and torturous word at a time. What should have taken an hour to read seemed as if it was taking a lifetime.

Once we finished, I couldn't help but wonder what everyone had thought of me. I imagined that I would never be asked to read a play again. Needless to say, I felt like a failure. I felt as if my acting career was over, a career that had barely started. Where do I go from here? If I can't read a play out loud, how in the world could I possibly act one out? As minutes went by, I finally caught my breath. I came to the realization that my intentions were to take their breath away with my acting skills; unfortunately, the only person whose breath was taken away was mine.

Ignoring what happened that day, I made the decision not to give up. You see, I lived on the same block as Culver Studios. The same movie studio where they filmed *Gone with the Wind*, *The Andy Griffith Show*, and *Lassie*, among other notable studio productions.

Well, every day I had to wake up and look outside my bedroom window and see this building that represented my hopes and dreams and think to myself, "Oh they ain't seen nothing yet! If they thought Hattie McDaniel, the first African American woman to win an Academy Award, for her role in *Gone with the Wind*, was amazing, just wait until they get a taste of Michelle Perdue!"

So, what did I do? Well, one day I decided that I had had enough. I found the courage to walk down the street to that studio so that I could be seen and heard. I was terrified. The whole time I walked down the street, I felt as if my cover could be blown at any moment. I looked good on the outside, but in the inside I was an emotional mess. I was full of self-doubt and overwhelmed with anxiety. However, just as I approached the gate, I thought to myself, "I know what I want. I want to get on that lot so that I can meet a casting director, and audition for a hit TV show. Then, something came over me. I got present, I felt grounded. I suddenly became intentional and deliberate about getting on that lot, but most importantly, I acted as if I deserved to be there and I took action. I told the security officer, who happened to be a woman, "Hi, my name is Michelle Perdue and I am here to meet with a casting director." I was firm, direct and confident.

The next thing I knew, the gate opened. "Really? Are you kidding me? Could life really be this good? This isn't Willy Wonka's chocolate factory and nor is she Willy Wonka, but I'll take it." Unfortunately, I looked around and didn't see a person in sight. At this point my heart's racing, my breathing is shallow, and my legs feel as if they could collapse at any moment. I went from feeling confident and excited to overwhelmed and confused. I wanted to give the appearance that I belonged there, but just before I had lost all hope, I looked to my right and saw a tall, slender young man taking out the trash. Needless to say, he was my saving grace. I immediately headed in his direction. I did everything I could to appear normal despite my erratic and frantic thoughts. I decided to approach him. I said, "Hi, I'm looking for the casting director's office, would you happen to know where I can find her?" He said, "No," but we started a great conversation.

I felt as though it was a dream come true. I finally made it on the studio lot. Then, the next thing I knew, I saw two men headed in my direction and no they weren't Oompa Loompas. They were, do I dare say it? Two security officers. I wanted to run and escape that dreadful and embarrassing moment, but I knew that wasn't the answer. Not only that, where was I going to run to, the end of the block? "Excuse me, Ma'am, what are you doing here?" Oh, who, me? Um…I was looking for a casting director's office, but… "Well, the security officer who let you on the lot made a mistake. This is her first day. This could actually get her fired." So there I was being escorted off the lot. I felt disappointed and humiliated, but at the end of the day, I made it to the other side of the gate all because I allowed myself to rise above my fears.

My experience left an imprint in my mind that will stay with me forever. It taught me that timing is everything and before you label yourself or your experience as a failure, know that just because you didn't succeed at that time, it doesn't determine who you will be. Today I am the happiest I have ever been. Because of some unsuccessful attempts in Los Angeles and the choices I've made to live a life of resilience, I am living my best life. My disappointments have given me the wisdom and fortitude to create my own platform to express my true self. Los Angeles by no means made me small. It only made my hopes and dreams bigger. It allowed me to recognize my strengths and appreciate my weaknesses. It taught me to discover who I really am and to me, that is worth a fortune.

Be You
Poem

I was surprised to realize all that I had inside, having to prove myself to Hollywood for the umpteenth time. Had to wait in line for my time to shine to prove to them that I was worth more than a dime. I said to myself let's stop and rewind wasting your time and mine.

No YOU take a seat, give me a chance to show you, a chance to be me, be free let me live out my dreams, don't try to overlook me because of something you can't see. I'm not a wannabe, I'm coming to you with originality. I was like a volcano that was just waiting to explode had so much inside of me didn't know how to let it go, let it flow, let it show, the fire oozing out of me.

Okay, let me stop and breathe release this tension inside of me, fears and all my anxieties, free myself from that stress feel blessed with all that God has given me. Now I can stop and exhale and smell the roses in life, by not getting caught up in the Hollywood hype you know not fitting their type. Too dark, too thin, not willing to sin, do anything to win just to fit in. I stood tall, embraced it all, rejection my lack of perfection, being told that I should take my life in another direction. Instead I listened to my inner voice and once I accepted it I had no choice. I rejoice today, because I am the woman that I always knew that I could be, I'm not asking for an approval because I know my destiny.

If you don't already know then let me explain, I was put on this earth to change things. You know, make a difference in the lives of people who have self-doubt God wanted me to share my stories my struggles he wanted me to reach out.

Now don't get confused, I'm not saying that I'm any better than you, God gave us all talents that he wanted us to use.
I'm not trying to abuse, but rather amuse you into believing the things you were born to do. See some people know their talents some don't some will discover them some won't.

I'm here today to say you don't have to settle for less, working a dead end job and not giving your best. I press to stress the importance of looking from within, stop listening to the world to find peace in your skin. I said stop listening to the world to find peace in your skin.

I know it's not easy to leap out on faith, afraid of the unknown thinking it's a mistake, so then you wait procrastinate afraid to live the truth, willing to compromise your dreams instead of being you. I want you to know I'm your cheerleader I'll encourage you if you fall. I'll be there to pick you up and help you stand tall. I want you to win that battle finish to the end. Be yourself and do you, never give in.

Re-Define Failure to Receive and Achieve Your Blessings

Failure is rooted in negativity and limitations due to its lack of depth and superficiality. As a result, it makes it challenging to see the benefits of failure and how it can alter your life in a meaningful and transformational way. It can create a disheartening illusion making you believe there's nothing to gain from your attempt to succeed at a desired goal or outcome. Unfortunately, this way of thinking can lead to a narrow point of view and consequently, limit your potential. Even more so, it could affect your motivation to even attempt to try new things that could potentially support your growth to rising and delivering your optimum performance.

I define failure as an undiscovered treasure hidden beneath the setbacks and disappointments of life waiting to be discovered so it can transform, enrich, and elevate your life. This definition inspires hope and provides a sense of personal empowerment. It gives you the opportunity to play an active role in your life. It breeds self-efficacy so that you establish some degree of control. The truth of the matter is the lesson and the re-framing of the concept of failure is worth its weight in gold. Why? Because it makes you feel as if you have control over what happens to you rather than feeling controlled by your circumstance. A circumstance that has the potential to liberate you and push you to step in the darkness of your fears so you can risk bigger, fail harder, and fear less.

Unfortunately, many people don't understand the broader and more comprehensive view of failure. Our society reinforces the notion that failure is a sign of weakness and instability. Consequently, to become successful or someone worthy of recognition, failures are hidden from the view of the world to protect one's anonymity and status. It's as if failure and success are unrelated; as if they are opposite one another and bear no connection whatsoever. The common belief is that failure and success should be disassociated from one another rather than working in unison to complement one another. This idea or way of thinking is the furthest from the truth. It's up to you to seek the truth and know that there is more than meets the eye.

Failure Isn't Personal; Let it Go to Let Yourself Shine

Often, people take failure personally and consequently, it defines who they are as a person. Instead of seeing the issue at hand as a lack of success they begin to view themselves as lacking success and therefore label themselves failures, further eroding their identity and self-esteem. If there is anything you take away from this chapter, please let it be the understanding that your failures do not define you. Your failures are not part of your genetic make-up, they are not part of your character, they do not determine the quality of your life, they can't hold you hostage without your compliance, nor do they define the meaning of your life unless you relinquish your inner power and forfeit your ability to see above and beyond it. Don't let your failures define you!

Your inability to succeed at a given task serves to inform you not of yourself, but rather how you have arrived at a particular outcome and what you need to do differently to have a better one. By keeping an open mind, your perception of failure helps you to see that it's more like your friend than it is your enemy. It's easy to fall into the trap of thinking failure is a bad thing, something to avoid at all costs or be ashamed of. Actually, it's quite the opposite!

If you come to understand failure as something that can inform you and give you a greater perspective of your outcome, much like a close friend, you will gain a greater appreciation for what it has to offer. Just think about it; a true friend is someone you can trust to tell you when you are doing right or wrong, which helps to inform you of your strengths and weaknesses. They are someone you can count on to guide you towards the right path, and they help you gain a sense of clarity. As you can see, the role of failure and our closest friends share similar qualities and are congruent in nature by giving us the opportunity to embrace new ways of thinking.

Failure is something that should be embraced. It's something we should come to expect as we travel the roads of life so we can influence our desired results with intention and shorten our learning curve by arriving at our destination sooner rather than later. The more we allow ourselves to fail and accept the realization of the true meaning of failure, the more quickly we can find a resolution to our problems. The more quickly we start seeing the results of our labor, the quicker we can pick ourselves up and move in the direction that will most likely maximize our growth and cultivate an optimum performance that elevates you, and ultimately, humanity.

We must allow ourselves to find comfort in our failure without becoming complacent. Accept that failure is part of our journey to success because without doing so, we stunt our growth and create a greater gap between where we are to where we want to be to challenge your failures and to hold yourself accountable for overcoming them you can begin by asking yourself these impactful questions.

- Where is the gap that lies in the midst of your shortcomings and may be getting in the way of you living fully and without regret?

> The more we allow ourselves to fail and accept the realization of the true meaning of failure, the more quickly we can find a resolution to our problems.

- In what ways have your failures strengthened and weakened you?

- How can you re-define your failures to make them work for you rather than against you?

I realize these questions may be easier to ask than to answer, which is why I have a greater appreciation for you if you are willing and courageous enough to go beyond the surface of your thoughts and ideas. This will allow you the opportunity to engage in self-exploration to find value in what appears to be a void in your life.

To be clear, a void in your life doesn't always signify something "bad" which could equate to you being a failure. Sometimes we resort to identifying ourselves as a failure when we are operating in the wrong season of change. Arielle Schwartz, author of *The Post-Traumatic Growth Guidebook*, says, "These seasons exist around you and in you. Once again, we see that each stage of growth has its own timing. Recognizing these rhythms and cycles can help you orient to the task of growth and change." This is very exciting news! It's exciting because it's a metaphor which explains how we are always at different phases in our lives. If we are at different phases and haven't yet reached our full bloom that would explain why we are not at our best at every beck and call. Maybe the reason you failed at a particular goal is simply because you are not in the right season to rise and shine and bloom to your potential.

Understanding Your Season of Change is Key

Sometimes, to overcome our failures we have to let go of things that stop us from rising and expressing ourselves truthfully. According to Schwartz, "Autumn can be seen as an invitation to let go and release that which no longer serves you." Therefore, if you are in this season of change maybe your failure has more to do with you needing to let go than your need to succeed. If this is the case, to move beyond your failure, it's essential that you come to the realization that you are not failing at a particular task, but rather it is failing you. It's failing you because it's time for you to cut ties and move on. This may be a good time for you to seize new opportunities and re-connect with your purpose.

At various points in our lives the need to quiet our inner critic becomes necessary for our health and well-being. We simply need to slow down to take in what we have been through, but also what we are going through. This season of change is related to winter. According to Schwartz, "Winter asks you to embrace the darkness and to reconnect internally with yourself." Therefore, maybe your failure is attributed to the need for you to slow down and allow for yourself to learn from your mistakes.

If you continue to press forward in spite of repeated rejection, an undeveloped skill-set, and a lack of awareness, without learning from it, it is inevitable you will continue to make the same mistake. This is a good time to reconnect, refresh and replace old people, places and things that do not serve you. Let the darkness remind you of your fears and vulnerabilities so that when light appears you emerge in the world renewed and restored. As long as you remember darkness isn't meant to be feared, but rather felt to expand your awareness of yourself, this season will have the potential to bless you with a harvest that could feed you emotionally and mentally for a lifetime.

The season of spring welcomes change. It's preparing you for new opportunities so that you can rise and shine to grow to your potential. According to Schwartz, "Spring invites you to plant new seeds and embrace the tender shoots of new growth." New growth is likely to happen after you have invested in your goals and you begin to reap the benefits of your labor. You planted the seeds of knowledge, you removed the weeds in your life that tried to deplete and disempower you. You nurtured your aspirations with resilience by weathering the storms. Now, you have put yourself in a position for optimal growth by turning your past failure into a success.

For so many of us, this is the season we most aspire to. It's the season that shows the rewards of our labor. It's what gave us the intrinsic and or extrinsic motivation to strengthen our shortcomings and attain our goals. Last, but certainly not least, it's the season of summer. According to Schwartz, "Summer provides an opportunity to expand into your full bloom." Who wouldn't like summer? Summer has a way of communicating to the world—you made it! You are at the top of your game. You overcame trials and tribulations. You lived in your best light and now you have bloomed into the true beauty you were always destined to be.

The next time you feel as though you have failed at any endeavor, goal, or task accept that maybe it's not your season to be in full bloom. Accept that where you are at in your journey to becoming… is where you are supposed to be. The seeds you planted yesterday will be a reflection of what you will produce tomorrow.

Time to Rise and Shine!

- *Redefine Failure*
  The way you define failure and the way it affects your life is a self-construct that is empowered by you. Only you can determine how your failure will impact you. Only you can redefine it's meaning to optimize your life so you can accomplish goals, achieve transformational breakthroughs and ignite the passion needed to rise and shine. Remember, it's not failure if you learn from your mistakes. Learning from your mistakes frees you from

self-deprecation, guilt, and shame. It changes your energy by refocusing your mind-set and allowing you to find the diamond in the rough that is rooted in negativity.

To redefine your failure start by analyzing your definition of failure; not the dictionaries' definition or my definition, but your definition. Write it down so that you have a visual representation of your perspective. As you read it, notice how it makes you feel. Does it inspire you? Does it boost your confidence to want to try again? Does it cause you to feel physically or emotionally stressed? Also, notice the words you've selected. Are they grounded in positivity? Do they instill hope? Or, do they deflate your ability to rise to face your fears and conquer your dreams? Once you analyze your definition, decide on what words support you and which ones suppress you. Then create a new one. Finally, when you have a definition that works for you choose an alternative course of action to help you achieve your goals.

- *Find Meaning in Everything*
  If you take the time to find meaning in everything that impacts you, it can be one of the greatest gifts you give to yourself. When you find meaning, particularly in things that wreak havoc in your life, you rob them of their energy and power. You rob them of having an opportunity to derail your ambitions, which have the potential to keep you emotionally stuck. For instance, when you find meaning in your "mess" you transcend beyond it to a higher consciousness which allows you to develop a healthier and more resilient way of being.

  To find meaning among the things that impact you identify those things in your life that are bigger than you. These things are not physically bigger than you but they are metaphorically bigger. Whatever they are, they are able to arouse you and expand you, allowing you to see and think differently. This allows you to detach yourself from them so that you have a greater appreciation not of the power you have over them, but rather the power they have over you. Another approach could simply be to strengthen your flexibility muscles. When you are flexible in your thinking by choosing to see your cup half full rather than half empty, you not only nurture a growth mindset, you plant seeds of resilience.

- *Develop A Sense of Gratitude*

When you can appreciate your failures and develop a sense of gratitude as a result of them, your failures can become one of the greatest assets to your life. Gratitude shows you are capable of seeing your failure with a healthy sense of being and emotional maturity. It allows you to validate those things that have hindered your progress yet helped you by providing life lessons. Gratitude has a way of restoring your faith in the midst of failure because it inspires you to see and believe what is possible.

You can develop an appreciation for gratitude by engaging your curiosity. Try not to allow yourself to be passive as it relates to the things that impact your life. When you ask the right questions, the right answers usually appear. However, the caveat to asking the right questions is knowing how to start. Start by asking questions that begin with *how* rather than *why*.

How questions give you access to a deeper understanding. For instance, consider questions such as, how can I turn this tragedy into a triumph? How can I rise and shine when my days are dark? Why questions tend to limit you, causing you to operate and think from a lower place within yourself. For instance, why me? Why now? These questions rob you of the resilience needed to transcend beyond a victim mentality. When you are curious and allow yourself the opportunity to appreciate life in all of its forms, it's like taking in a breath of fresh air. It rejuvenates you and creates a sense of balance in your life that would otherwise not be possible.

Chapter 7

BE BRAVE; VALIDATE YOUR VISION

Your vision will become clear only when
you can look into your own heart.
Who looks outside, dreams; who looks inside, awakes.
Carl Jung

L ost dreams, poor self-esteem, dope fiends' babies left unclean, these are the unsightly things I see. Whatever happened to how things used to be? When we treated the elderly with the utmost respect, didn't sell drugs on the corner but earned an honest paycheck. Where you didn't have to sleep with one eye open, lookin' out for the police prayin' and hopin.'

I had no idea these words were like seeds planted in the depths of my mind and simply needed to be nurtured to be brought to life. I had no idea that they would give my life such powerful meaning. It all started in Los Angeles when I was attending the Ruskin School of Acting. I had an opportunity to audition for the *Vagina Monologues*, written by Eve Ensler. The play is comprised of various monologues regarding the sexual experiences and body images of women. I was thrilled to have the opportunity to play one of the characters. I never knew that this experience would be the catalyst for me wanting to write my own poetry to inspire and elevate the humanity in others.

The day of the audition, I decided to do something that was courageous and unthinkable. I decided to write and perform a poem about my vagina, yes, my vagina. It was titled, "A Vagina Without a Voice" and it was empowering! I was liberated and the best part was, it was my story. A story relating to my experience with my father. - I had buried this story so deep within me that when I shared it, it seemed as if the weight of the world had been lifted from my shoulders. No longer was the pain of my past holding me captive, but little did I know, this was just the beginning of my poetic journey.

I remember the day I shared my poem with my acting teacher. A teacher who created a safe platform for us students to confront our fears to live and act authentically in the moment. There were many times we laughed and cried together as we trained to become actors. It was because of his guidance and his approach to the craft of acting, I felt it was safe to be me. However, I was still a bit nervous. I wasn't sure if I was ready to share a part of my voice I had just discovered. Fortunately, to my surprise I felt as if I had discovered a jewel, but didn't realize the magnitude of its worth. I knew that it had value, but to what degree? I wasn't sure. What I did know was that I felt as if I had accomplished something bigger than my fears, bigger than myself.

On the other hand, reading it out loud brought its own challenges. This would be the first time I would say the word vagina in a public space. Initially, the word caused a sense of unease and made me feel self-conscious. The word made me feel like a thief, meaning it didn't belong to me. As if it was foreign and I didn't have any relationship with it whatsoever. As if my vagina owned me rather than me owning it, causing me to feel powerless and disconnected. However, the more I read the poem the more I began to embrace the word and attach meaning to it. I began to feel more comfortable in my skin. I began to see my vagina as part of my being in a way that I hadn't acknowledged it before. The more I read the poem the more I felt as if my vagina was coming to life. I had allowed myself to embrace my vulnerability to speak my truth and honor it to the fullest. After reading the poem to my teacher, he made me feel supported. He made me feel as if my words mattered and they were worthy of recognition. He then suggested that I turn my poem into a one-woman show. On the inside, I was ecstatic and overflowing with excitement. I felt heard and because of that I knew I had to keep going.

Over the years, I began to write more poetry. I enjoyed it so much that I would find myself performing at various venues in Los Angeles. There was something about performing poetry that made me feel as if something magical was happening inside me, but even more so, outside of me. For instance, it made me feel as if something spiritual was transpiring where I was so connected to the world and the people in it that I felt an adrenaline rush so big I could move mountains. It was as if I was one with the universe. There was no worry, fear, or regrets. It was just me and my words falling on the ears of those who were willing to listen.

Today, I have come to accept that I have a special relationship with writing and performing poetry. A relationship that I have come to embrace with all of my being. It took some time to realize that the love I have for poetry was going to be bigger than myself. I had no idea that it would be a vehicle to transport my most profound and intimate thoughts to my audience. To date, I have used my poetry to inspire business professionals, community leaders, youth, church goers, and most recently cancer survivors.

At the beginning of the COVID-19 outbreak, I found myself writing poetry for cancer survivors as a way of being productive and doing something I was passionate about. It resulted in a poetry CD titled, *Resilient I Am*. It has proved to be something I am very proud of and I hope that it will reach many far and wide. When my friend and fellow cancer survivor told me the impact the CD had on her life, I was beyond thrilled. She truly made my heart smile.

I now feel as if my passion for poetry and my ability to incorporate it into my presentations gives my life new meaning. I'm not just writing about my vagina, I'm writing about things that facilitate transformational breakthroughs that make people's spirits rise and fill them with confidence and conviction. I am encouraging others to use their voices to validate their stories, to confront their self-limiting thoughts, and empower their words.

Before I moved to Los Angeles in 2001, I would have never known how poetry would have made such a difference in my life. I couldn't see all the parts of my vision in order for me to fully see the value in it. However, over the years, I was able to connect the dots and truly understand the meaning behind it. Therefore, now that I can see more clearly, I am able to shine much brighter as I seek to own and act on my purpose. So, keep an open mind and know that your vision may come to you in parts. It's your patience and understanding that will make your vision whole, one revelation and one discovery at a time.

Become a Visionary to See the Riches of Your Potential

Chances are, at some point in your life, you've had dreams. It's also a good chance that as you dreamt, you visualized magical moments of pure bliss. There are some who hold on to their dreams in spite of the highs and lows of life and take the necessary actions to make them a reality. They've allowed their vision to give them the inspiration needed to go beyond visualizing to actually living it. It's because of their focus and relentless determination that they endure the hardships of life while pursuing their goal, which requires commitment and an intentional mind-set.

The word *action* is one of the most powerful words in the dictionary. In addition to bringing our visions to reality, it also enriches our lives in other ways. It allows us to discover what does and does not work throughout all facets of our lives. It informs us as we travel life's journey by providing a sense of direction to become better human beings. In addition, taking action not only has the ability to save your life, it also has the ability to save others. Therefore, it should not be underestimated. It must be taken into consideration at all times; without it, dreams will die, mankind will cease to exist, and nature will fail to thrive beyond recognition.

Action is essential to manifesting our visions and living in a world that helps us to survive as well as thrive. Are you taking action to bring your vision to reality, or have you become so attached to your vision that you are not willing to go beyond it? Maybe now it resembles a repeated episode in your mind that continues to capture your imagination, yet holds you captive. It has tricked you into believing that you will live out your dreams if only you continue to fantasize and visualize your desires. However, research and those who have achieved any kind of notable success have shown us time and time again that if you want to accomplish anything in life, it requires action. Simply wishing and hoping won't do.

Seeing Your Vision is Not Enough

Those who get caught up and remain stuck in the seeing and not the doing will unfortunately compromise their dreams, vision, and ultimately their purpose. Why? Because they have allowed themselves to lose focus and be misguided by the lure of life's instant gratifications. They have succumbed to the temptations of life's pleasures and all the good things they have to offer. I am here to encourage you to hold on just a little while longer. Trust that your vision has the ability to allow you to see bigger and better days. Trust that it can transform your life from ordinary to extraordinary by allowing you to live fully and without regrets. Trust that by validating your vision and acting on faith, you are less likely to make a mistake. Mistakes are often made when we don't trust that our dreams and visions serve a purpose. When we ignore them, we are bound to settle for things that are less fruitful and meaningful to the evolution of our spirit.

It's important that you allow yourself to visualize your dreams in the most intimate and detailed way as long as you don't live solely in that space. This can lead to unproductiveness. Having and maintaining clarity for your vision is one of the most meaningful gifts you can give to yourself. For instance, as you visualize, try to notice your emotions, actions and environment.

- Are you by yourself or are you among a group of people?
- Are you smiling and do you appear to be filled with joy and excitement or do you appear to be relaxed and deep in thought?
- Notice where you are. Is it a place that's recognizable or is it new and unfamiliar?

The more clarity you have, the more likely your vision will become a reality because it has more meaning. Clarity enhances your emotional connection and gives you something to hold on to when life seems to be working against you rather than for you. As a result, it gives you more of an incentive to not only see, but to live the best life possible.

As you take action into consideration for bringing your vision to fruition, it's also essential to consider other factors that may hinder your success. Although the fruits of your labor will be worthy of your efforts, there is also a price to pay. For instance, you want to keep an open mind by understanding that everyone won't see or buy in to your vision. There are times when you may feel compelled to justify your vision to others simply to satisfy their judgements so you can feel validated. This is a trap you want to avoid. The only person who needs to validate your vision is you. Your vision is meant to be seen by you; that's why others can't see it unless, of course, you share it with them. Needless to say, don't let yourself become argumentative or bitter with those who feel your vision is out of reach or unrealistic. They don't have the power and nor should they to determine what you see or who you should be.

When You Own Your Vision You Maximize Your Potential

Use your power to own every part of your vision and protect it with all of your being. Be proud of it, let it live within the most nurturing space of your mind, heart, and soul; don't be afraid to let the world know it. I know it's not always easy, especially when the world is so good at putting restrictions and boundaries on your potential due to your age, race, religion, and everything in between. However, your vision isn't meant to be a secret. It shouldn't be hidden in the shadows of our fears and insecurities. It needs to breathe. It needs exposure and attention to guide and inspire you by helping you to live with purpose and in prosperity and in doing so, it will inspire others.

A word of caution: as your vision takes form you may come to realize that what you see is not always what you get. Sometimes, your vision may present itself like a physical product where some parts

> The only person who needs to validate your vision is you. Your vision is meant to be seen by you; that's why others can't see it unless, of course, you share it with them.

are sold separately; meaning, your vision is incomplete and therefore you must wait until the other pieces are present in order for it to be effective and reach its maximum potential. Keep in mind that this concept is not meant to discourage or confuse you. In time, it can prove to be your saving grace. It is meant to broaden your way of seeing and thinking so that your vision is more inclusive and creates room for endless possibilities. Therefore, as your vision comes to light it may be part of something much greater than itself. Something that will allow you to live a richer and more meaningful life. It's for this reason alone that you don't want to be so quick to abandon it when you find yourself taking a different path in life than expected. Hold on to your vision and take results driven actions to reveal its true purpose and intentions.

Time to Rise and Shine!

- *Believe Your Vision Can Become a Reality*
  In order for your vision to become a reality you must believe that one day it will manifest. You must believe that with the necessary actions you have some control over the outcome to bring it to fruition. It's the belief in your vision that will develop the mental toughness needed for you to go the distance and overcome barriers. However, you must first conceptualize your vision and believe it can become a reality. Napoleon Hill once said, "Whatever the mind of man can conceive and believe, it can achieve." The question is, once you believe in your vision, how do you keep it alive?

  You can keep your vision alive with your ability to be creative and through self-expression. For instance, you can create a vision poster to help reinforce your vision. This way, if your vision begins to fade, you can look at your poster and rely on it to give you inspiration, but also remind you of why you do what you do. To create a poster, Kamran Akbarzadeh, founder of Dream Achievers Academy suggests you first create a vision statement. Next, identify key words and statements to capture a mental image. Link them together to create a mental picture. Then, draw or paint what you have in mind. Finally, have a professional painter or graphic designer paint what you have drawn. Include the written details as well.

He also suggests you make a video of your vision. I believe making a video is another great way to reinforce your vision to serve as a reminder of why you do what you do. In this case, you have an opportunity to literally say it. You can discuss not only your "why" for pursing your vision, but you can also discuss the specific action steps you plan to take to make it a reality. Once you make the video, feel free to watch it anytime you want to be inspired or to get others to invest in it.

- ## *Let Your Fear Ignite Your Vision*
  The fire you have within you is what keeps you invested and connected to your vision. It's that burning feeling you experience that gets you up and moving towards your goals. It is derived from an organic place within yourself and can be used as a navigation system to help keep you on track. Oftentimes, this is how we know if our vision is worth investing our resources in simply because of the way our vision makes us feel. However, fear, which serves as a primal function and is a necessary emotion, can sabotage our vision if we are not careful.

  If you sense that fear is beginning to take over, rather than ignore it, have the courage to face it. You face it by becoming aware of its presence. Once you are aware, make it a point to re-connect with your vision by listening to what your fear is telling you or not telling you. Our fear has a way of not being truthful; it only tells us part of the story. Therefore, it's easy for fear to reveal your weaknesses while concealing information about your strengths. Your goal is to identify the difference.

Fear can communicate negative statements, such as, "You're not good enough. You're wasting your time. Who do you think you are? You come from nothing therefore you are nothing." These are all statements that must be reframed to support you and your vision. Find the positive in the negative by responding in such a way that you feel empowered and inspired to realize your vision. For instance, "I am not wasting my time. Anything that has to do with me bringing my vision to reality is time well spent, thank you." You want to know who I think I am? I am not my fears, my flaws or my failures. I am somebody. Somebody worthy of love, success and freedom so that I can be me and rise above you. Finally, after you put fear in its place continue to take strategic and deliberate actions to make your vision a reality. Never forget your vision is worth it and so are you.

- *Stay Focused and Keep Your Eyes on the Prize*
  When you are focused and are able to keep your eyes on the prize you're less likely to experience interference with your vision. Focus allows you to prioritize your tasks so that when you are faced with distractions that aren't beneficial or relevant to the attainment of your goals, you are able to avoid them and/or put them in perspective. Furthermore, by maintaining a sense of focus, you save precious time because you are able to achieve your goals at a much faster pace. Therefore, try to be aware of your time. It is one of the most valuable assets you have as a human being. Once you are depleted of time, there is no point of

return. Although this idea may seem like common sense to many, it's taken for granted by many more.

You can keep your eyes on the prize by giving your attention to things that really matter. Things that have the potential to change the trajectory of your life. It's a matter of weighing the cost versus the rewards. Do you know where you are spending your time? Jack Canfield, author of *The Success Principles*, identifies one of his core principles as, "Say No To The Good So That You Can Say Yes To The Great." This means that every opportunity that is available to you is not for you. You want to be selective in where you focus your time and energy. To account for where you are spending your time, he suggests making a list of your opportunities by listing the good opportunities on one side and the great opportunities on the other. Next, seek out advisors to help you evaluate your potential pursuits. Then, test the waters to see if it's worth your investment. Finally, take time to reflect on where you are spending your time. The good will keep you satisfied, but it's the great that will bring you the greatest success.

Chapter 8

FIND THE SHINE IN YOUR WHINE

Be thankful for what you have; you'll end up having more.
If you concentrate on what you don't have,
you will never, ever have enough.
Oprah Winfrey

Years ago, I gave birth to a beautiful and healthy baby boy. He was the son that I had always dreamed of, full of life and vulnerability. He depended on his father and me for his every need. Soon after he was born, my husband and I moved from Los Angeles to Minneapolis. We were thrilled at the thought of buying our first home and raising our son. Initially we rented a two bedroom apartment until we found the home we had hoped and prayed for. However, it seemed as if before we could even get the baby bed unpacked, I received a disturbing call from my mother, saying "Michelle, I found a lump in my breast. I can't get in to see a doctor for nearly two months." I was terrified.

In the past, my mother has been accused on various occasions of being overly dramatic with the potential to take things out of proportion. I believe her desire to magnify or over-exaggerate particular events stems from her innate ability for telling stories. However, from the sound of her voice, I knew this was different. I could hear the fear in her voice and feel the weight of her sigh as it knocked me down like a heap of waves forcing me to the shallow floor of the ocean. At that moment, I wanted to be indulged with her sense of humor, a personality trait many of us family members have come love, which was now as dry as sand. Consequently, I suddenly became aware of the seriousness of the matter. I sat at my computer desk motionless and afraid with endless thoughts running through my mind.

Why was this happening now? This was supposed to be one of the happiest moments of my life. Without hesitation, I asked my mother, "If I find you a doctor here in Minnesota, would you go?" Without question, she agreed. Not fully realizing the changes that were about to take place, I welcomed my mother to our Minnesota home with open arms.

Soon after her arrival, we learned she tested positive for breast cancer. We went from being hopeful to uncertain, all within a matter of minutes. I remember it just as if it were yesterday. Tears streaming down my mother's face as she received her test results over the phone. It was confirmed that she had breast cancer. I did my best to stay as strong as I could. I wanted to be a pillar of strength for my mother, but even for me, it was hard to bear. Seeing my mother deeply distraught and in search of answers made me feel powerless. I felt as if nothing I could say in that moment would bring her the comfort she needed to regain her inner strength. She cried and so did I.

I found myself whining to God and wondering how we were going to get through this difficult time. A time of fear and sacrifice. For instance, I was supporting my cancer stricken mother during sub-zero weather conditions in Minnesota while simultaneously meeting the needs my new infant son. Why? I just didn't understand. I was confused and disappointed. Not disappointed in my mother, but in the unforeseen circumstance, which seemed to be robbing me of an experience of a lifetime. It was the experience of me giving my son all the love and attention he needed to thrive as a normal, healthy human being.

It wasn't until later on that I had an opportunity to sit down and reflect on that life-changing year my mother spent with us. The more I reflected, the more I realized how lucky I was during that trying time. See, what you don't know is my mother had a long history of substance abuse and as a result, she wasn't always capable of being the mother she could have been. Over the years, she missed special occasions and turn down opportunities that could have potentially strengthened our relationship. It was heartbreaking, to say the least. Now, with my mother living with us it turned out to be time well spent, which meant the world to me. For instance, I would often invite my mother to come and listen to me perform poetry at a local café. Having my mother in the audience was bittersweet. I felt supported and excited to feel and see her presence, but it wasn't always easy to tell my stories. These were stories that were told in the form of poetry that expressed my pain and opened old wounds, yet inspired others to live their lives unapologetically.

The best part of having my mother in the audience was hearing her feedback afterwards. Despite what she had been through or what she had put us through growing up, she owned it. She never made excuses for the choices she made. She never once made me feel ashamed to express my poetic voice. I would like to think that my poetry bonded us in a way that my words in a casual conversation couldn't. As if poetry was something she could relate to coming from a storyteller to a storyteller. Poetry appeared to unite us rather than divide us. Was it because my poetry filled mental gaps that enabled her to see herself from a different perspective so that she more fully understood the repercussions of her actions? Was it because I was never brought up to honor and validate my voice and now that I am, she has an appreciation for it? Or, was it because there were strangers in the audience who were inspired by my poetry? They wanted to live bigger and more fulfilling lives and because of that, she was inspired to do the same? What I do know is, the time we spent together was much bigger than cancer. It was bigger than us. It's for this reason I learned a great deal about my mother and myself during this trying time.

If I had spent less time whining to God and questioning his intentions, I believe I would have come to appreciate the situation a lot sooner. I would have had a greater appreciation for the wonderful moments we shared by simply getting to know my mother as a person and connecting emotionally on a much deeper and authentic level. I would have taken more photos of her daily transformations to reveal her strengths while she was going through chemotherapy. This would have allowed me to capture her courage and commitment to wanting to stay alive.

Today I am beyond grateful for sharing that experience with my mother. I believe I learned more about her in that year than I did in all the previous years up to that point and it was worth it. She taught me the true meaning of perseverance, courage, and how to find the shine in my whine. I believe it's when we find the shine in our whine that we give ourselves a gift that is priceless, character building, and emotionally rewarding. We just need to take the time to recognize it. And when we do, we must seize the moment by living in it and embracing it.

Learn to Embrace the Good, the Bad and the Ugly

Sometimes in the midst of our despair and feelings of hopelessness we find it difficult to see and feel beyond our present circumstances. We become consumed and fixated on events that rob us from appreciating all the gifts that life has to offer. Gifts that if recognized and embraced would teach us life lessons, change the scope and dynamics of our lives, and provide the fuel we need to live in abundance, as well as the emotional and mental clarity to welcome new opportunities. Unfortunately, when life begins to take its toll, our vision can become distorted and our world narrowed, causing us to feel a multitude of emotions. These emotions include but certainly are not limited to frustration and resentment.

If we are not careful, we can begin to whine and complain about things that are going wrong in our lives without taking into consideration what could be going right. We focus on what we don't have without realizing what we do have. Have you ever met such a person? Or know someone in your family who fits the description? No matter how bright the sun shines, they somehow manage to find a storm brewing amongst the clouds. In such cases, we must challenge and acknowledge our circumstance with an open-mind and heart. This will enable us to reap the benefits of life's lessons to deliver a meaningful and highly celebrated performance.

We must have faith in our humanity. We must believe that despite what we are going through, whether it's grieving, engaging in self-destructive behavior, or feeling let down or put down, there is something to be taken from our life experiences. Even when we feel emotionally and spiritually bankrupt, we must strive to be curious and dedicated to learning about ourselves in every way possible. We owe it to ourselves to operate from the highest part of our being and

> We must have faith in our humanity. We must believe that despite what we are going through, whether it's grieving, engaging in self-destructive behavior, or feeling let down or put down, there is something to be taken from our life experiences.

when we view our circumstances from multiple perspectives that is exactly what we are doing. Essentially, this concept is based on the idea of learning to find the shine in your whine.

Finding the Shine in Your Whine Takes Work

The shine is that person, place or thing that has the potential to alter the course of your life experiences so that you can rise and elevate your performance in a way that captures the essence of your best self. However, like a diamond in the rough, it waits to be discovered by someone who possesses the quality of patience or has the ability to view the world as though it were a Picasso painting, causing you to look deeper at an abstracted view in search of meaning and its value. When you discover its purpose and can make sense of its existence, you welcome it in your life because you can see the value and joy it can bring no matter how big or small. What matters is your willingness to entertain the thought of something good coming from something that is perceived to be bad. Thus reframing it so that it works to your advantage in helping you to become a stronger and wiser human being.

- When was the last time you found the shine in your whine and how did it impact your life?
- What adverse circumstances are you currently facing that would benefit from you finding the shine in your whine?
- Do you have a tendency to whine about the cards you've been dealt in the game of life without finding some form of gratitude?

As you answer these questions you may have greater clarity in how you process particular experiences yet are unclear about the origins of your negative thoughts. There is a concept known as negativity bias, which explains why you are more likely to focus on those things that are emotionally taxing rather than emotionally satisfying. Negativity bias is an evolutionary function that our ancestors relied on to keep them out of harm's way. It's what they relied on for dodging the misfortunes of life and for survival. Fortunately, today we are not dependent on this function in the same way our ancestors were.

Our brain naturally scans for negative stimuli, because we are more likely to be impacted by things that are perceived as negative as opposed to positive. For instance, if you gave a presentation and afterwards received 30 evaluations and out of 30 evaluations, three people gave you low scores and that is what you focused on, this would be an example of negativity bias. For this reason Rick Hanson, author of *Resilient* says, "Our brains are like Velcro for bad experiences but Teflon for good ones." Therefore, we want to be conscious and embrace open mindedness to better process our perceptions. Otherwise, you will be forced to see things not as they are, but rather things that are based on selective criteria. Needless to say, when you seek to gravitate and have a propensity towards negativity, your performance suffers. Your bias that's rooted in negativity serves as a disservice to you. To further illustrate this concept, let's look at it from the perspective of an actor.

Imagine if actors only agreed to portray characters when they felt they possessed the same life experiences as the character they are tasked to bring to life. More specifically, what if an actor was given the role of a character who was diagnosed with cancer yet the actor themselves had never had this experience and the only thing they kept telling themselves was, "I am not a cancer patient. How could I possible play this character? This character is so far from who I am as a person that I can't relate." The first thing I would say to this person is, "How unfortunate. You have an enormous opportunity to not only grow as an actor, but even more so, as a human being. This could be your blessing in disguise!"

Risk-Taking is Valuable and Necessary

This is your chance to find the shine in your whine. Your performance is only as good as the risks you are willing to take and you can't take risks when you play it safe. Therefore, rather than looking at this situation from a place of insufficient means, look at it from a place of abundance and curiosity. Acknowledge it for its potential and the value it brings. By taking this approach, it forces the actor to search within themselves to find commonality between themselves and the character rather than the actor shutting down and feeling as though they can't relate. When the actor does find a way to relate to the character, the actor and the character they are portraying become intertwined which is necessary for the character to come to life. It's about give and take, and giving up some aspects of who you have identified yourself to be in the best interest of serving the role. You can't do that if you aren't willing to see beyond the scope of your experiences, the limitations of your mind-set, and the impact of your personal values.

Time to Rise and Shine!

- *Stop Before You Are Emotionally and Spiritually Depleted*
  Stop investing your time, thoughts, and energy into things that will only leave you emotionally and spiritually bankrupt, causing you to feel depleted or insufficient. Your need to settle for life's misfortunes and heartbreaks without acknowledging the gifts that it also brings only perpetuates a cycle of fear and lack of emotional stability. You were born with the inherent ability to master and live beyond the inevitable storms of life. Therefore, by stepping up and stopping this cycle you interrupt the habitual practice of whining about things that render you powerless. You are powerful beyond measure.

To stop means you allow yourself to be in the moment by asking yourself relevant and thought provoking questions that lead to optimism and positive thinking. Such as, "What thoughts are running through my mind at this very moment that are delaying or distorting the perception of my circumstance? What type of emotions am I feeling and how do they impact my life? What story am I telling myself that keeps me invested in negativity?" When you allow yourself to focus on the past or future, you rob yourself of the opportunity to answer these questions. Unfortunately, during these moments, fear taints our thought process. Fear stagnates the progression of our potential while disguising itself as a mother figure by trying to protect you and keep you out of harm's way. We must be diligent to replenish our mind and spirit with positive thoughts so we become empowered to act responsibly in how we will interpret our situation.

As you stop to analyze the situation at hand, keep in mind that it is okay to allow yourself to feel human emotions, particularly in the face of adversity. Such as fear, anger and sadness. The ability to find the shine in your whine is not about avoiding these feelings or feeling guilty if you can't avoid them. It's about allowing yourself to have an open mind and coming to the realization of how you can use that experience to advance your life in spite of fear, anger and sadness. It's when we lose sight of the things that truly matter and buy into the things that don't that we get tunnel vision and decrease our chances of seeing the potential goodness that surrounds us and resides within us. So, if you are one of those people who sets boundaries on your interpretations of life, today is your day to stop the whining and complaining in order to discover what awaits you. You have the ability to see above and beyond your circumstance; you have the ability to stop the whine and bring the shine to raise your potential.

- *When in Doubt Look for Clarity*

  Look at your circumstance from an objective point of view rather than a subjective point of view. All too often, when we are dealing with life-altering situations that are emotionally charged we don't see things as they really are. What we think we see is simply not what is. We see things through a lens that reflects our values and beliefs without taking into consideration factual information. As a result, the appearance of our circumstance becomes overshadowed by our emotions and opinions.

  You owe it to yourself to have a sense of clarity about your gifts or the shine in your whine. When you have clarity, you see there is a gift waiting to be discovered, you see the gift belongs to you and you deserve it, and you see that this is a learning opportunity that could potentially change the course of your life. However, you must allow yourself to be vulnerable by stepping outside of your comfort zone and trusting there will be brighter days. This trust and belief in yourself breeds confidence and gives you the wings and inner strength needed to soar and become a better you.

  Patrick Overton once said, "When you walk to the edge of all the light you have and take that first step into the darkness of the unknown, you must believe that one of two things will happen: There will be something solid for you to stand upon or you will be taught how to fly." Are you ready to fly? Are you ready to see what's on the other side of the cliff? Are you ready to face your fears so that you can experience all the gifts that life has to offer? Or will you stand there as you watch your life pass you by wondering how different things could have been if only you were courageous enough to see what was possible? The power lies within you. You get to decide.

- ## *Be Patient to Discover Your Shine*

   Patience is key to finding the shine in your whine. The gifts you discover may not arrive right when you want them to. Sometimes, it may take days, months, or years to gain clarity in knowing why you were faced with a particular challenge, what were you supposed to take away from it and how it's supposed to benefit you in the future. It may take other encounters and experiences during your lifetime to connect the dots. This process may help you to make sense of what you went through so that you can have a better appreciation for your hardships. Needless to say, your gift may seem illogical at the time.

   To be patient in the most productive way means that you are not passively patient, but are actively patient. Passively patient means you are not intentional about engaging in self-discovery. You are not actively considering all the goodness that life has to offer. You can't always see beyond your fears, flaws and failures. Furthermore, when you are passively patient in finding the shine in your whine you are more likely to engage in compulsive thinking which could ultimately lead to compulsive behavior. Furthermore, patience that results in passive behavior keeps you subconsciously blinded to lessons to be learned, weaknesses that are in need of strengthening, and strengths that could be capitalized on to enhance your growth. On the other hand, when you are active with your patience you are not mentally stuck on things that prevent you from finding the good in what could be perceived as bad. You're not waiting for someone to come and relieve or rescue you. You proceed with your life by believing at some point in time that experience will serve you for the better rather than for the worse. You will become conscious of the ways in which you tell your story about the challenges you have been through. Consequently, you will appear to look more like a resilient and courageous individual rather than a victim of your circumstances.

When you are actively patient and tell your story to others with empowered words, you also want to communicate to yourself with words that will inspire and uplift you. For instance, you say to yourself, "I want more out of life. I know there is something better for me and the only thing that separates me from living the life I want are my limited perspectives. I will not let my perceptions dictate my destiny. I will live empowered and immerse my thoughts and ideas in positivity. I will become an investigator, interrogator, and manipulator by seeking the true gifts that lie beneath my circumstance. Then, I will rise and allow myself to step up so I can show up in the world victorious and brave." Regardless of the words you choose, try to feel them and not just say them. It's in the feeling of the words that you will cultivate an experience that is not only memorable, but magical.

Chapter 9

SURVIVE THE UNEXPECTED

Where do we enroll in Life 101?
Where are the classes dealing with the loss of a job,
the death of a loved one, the failure of a relationship?
Unfortunately, those lessons are mostly learned
through trial by fire and the school of hard knocks.
Les Brown

It was a new year, a new day, a new me, and I was feeling good. It was January 2017 and I was determined to face my fears and do things I had never done before. I had decided I was going to make inspirational videos and share my message with the world. I wanted to empower others to not only follow their dreams, but to dream bigger and take action as a result of them. I felt liberated because I gave myself permission to fail. What I didn't realize was that my failures needed to be kept in perspective. I quickly learned that when your life is at stake failure can disappoint you, but it doesn't necessarily jeopardize your life. Well, the day came when I felt as if failure had taken a back seat to my need to stay alive.

"Are you sure you have the right person?" This is the thought that came to mind as I listened to this unfamiliar, yet calming and sympathetic voice at the other end of my phone. "Yes, we would like for you to come in for more imaging and three biopsies. One biopsy on one breast and two on the other. It could be calcifications, or it could be cancer." Are you kidding me? I was shocked as I heard these words. My legs weakened. My eyes glazed over with tears. My voice softened as I began to be consumed by my emotions. My head was no longer in that moment. I began thinking about my life and the end of it. What if I have cancer? What does that mean for my kids, my husband, my hopes and dreams? I wanted answers. I wanted to be reassured at that moment that I was going to be okay.

Immediately after the call, with tears streaming down my face, I called my husband at work and told him it was possible that I may have breast cancer. He was my saving grace. He tried to calm me down and reassured me that everything was going to be okay. The minutes that it took for him to get home felt like a lifetime. In retrospect, I am relieved that he was at work and my two children were at school. I was a nervous wreck. I paced the floors. I cried out loud. I talked to myself as I searched for answers. It was Monday and waiting two additional days for my doctor's appointment had proven to be even more challenging. Not only was I on pins and needles waiting for an answer and feeling tormented by the suspense, but I still had work to do.

The next day was my daughter's 7th birthday and we were planning to give her a birthday party at home. It was a time for celebration. The energy which exuded from my soon-to-be 7-year old daughter and my 9-year old son was amplified with excitement and anticipation. They knew mom could give a good party and they were ready. However, under the circumstance of feeling consumed by the recent news, the very thought of kids screaming and running through the house brought its own stress. I did everything I could to appear as if everything was okay. I gave hugs when I wanted to push away. I played games when I wanted to be alone. I smiled when I wanted to cry. At times it felt as if I were having an out of body experience. As if I were going through the motions, yet I wasn't fully part of the experience because my mind was somewhere else. However, it was important to me that I didn't worry the kids. I felt as if they needed me and the truth of the matter was, I needed them. Therefore, I did the best I could to be the best mom I could.

The day for my biopsies finally arrived. I was a nervous wreck to say the least. I knew that it wouldn't be a walk in the park, and it was both physically and emotionally draining. I did my best to remain patient as my breasts were being pulled and poked with needles. I distinctly remember not receiving enough anesthesia for my left breast and feeling the tissue being ripped from my body—I screamed. It was incredibly painful and I wanted it to stop. However, in my heart, I knew that stopping was not an option. Fortunately, I was given more numbing medication to rectify the problem. Little did I know, this would prove to be the beginning of unforeseen and painful complication. Immediately after the biopsy, my right breast started to bleed uncontrollably. My nurse instantly took action and began to put pressure on it. It was obvious that she knew what she was doing and that she had done this before. No pun intended, but she made me feel as if I was in good hands. I was afraid. I did everything that was asked of me. I wanted to appear brave and strong, but on the inside I was doing everything I could to not fall apart.

After meeting with my doctor a couple of days later, it was confirmed; I had breast cancer. I was told that I had breast cancer not only in one breast, but both. I was devastated. My world had suddenly been turned upside down. I can only imagine that my mother had felt the same way. The good news was that I was diagnosed initially as a stage 0, which is considered to be the earliest form of breast cancer. Also, after additional testing, it was later revealed that my lymph nodes were unaffected by the cancer. It all appeared to be contained within my milk ducts. I was so relieved. As a result, there was no talk of radiation or chemotherapy. The plan according to my knowledge, was to simply do a lumpectomy. I can live with that, I thought. Go in, get the cancer out, and then go on about my life as usual, right? Wrong.

It was Friday. My kids and I desperately wanted to do something fun and exciting. So, what better thing to do in Minnesota during the middle of winter? Go to the Mall of America! The indoor amusement park always seems to be a magnet for the kids, they enjoy the rides. This was also during a time when the stress level at home was high. Being in a different environment and seeing them happy meant more to me than ever. Hearing the continuous screams and laughter in the midst of a sea of children somehow seemed comforting. I believe they helped to remind me what life is truly about: living in the moment and enjoying life to the fullest.

Some kids approached the rides looking uncertain and afraid, but they did it anyway. Some kids waited in long lines to get on a ride only to be cut off and told the ride is full and they would have to wait longer, but they stayed and did it anyway. They knew what they had to do in order to get on that ride and it's a good chance they thought, "Well, I've come this far, so why give up now?" It's amazing what children can teach us when we open our eyes and appreciate the simplicities of life, but more importantly, the meaning behind them.

As the kids and I walked through the park, eagerly looking for the next thrilling ride, my cell phone rang. It was my doctor. I could tell by the sound of her voice something wasn't right. She began to inform me about the results of my lumpectomy surgery. She told me she needed to remove significantly more tissue than expected and she never found a clear margin. She said that even thought it was contained within my milk ducts, it sprouted out in many directions, similar to a tree branch. Then to make matters worse, she recommended that I have a double mastectomy, the removal of both of my breasts. I went from feeling devastated when I initially found out I had cancer, to shocked, angry, and confused.

There were times when I felt speechless and found it difficult to breathe. I don't know which was spinning faster, the rides or my head as I tried to bring myself to terms with what was being said. I thought to myself, how could this be? This is not supposed to be happening. I was diagnosed as a stage 0 for goodness sake...seriously? Once I realized the seriousness of the matter, I did my best to immediately collect my kids and run to the nearest place I could find that would allow me to have some privacy; that place was the restroom stall. I cried uncontrollably. Once again my husband soon came to the rescue.

Now it's time for surgery. I've accepted the realities of my circumstance and I'm ready to engage in the next phase of my journey of healing and overcoming cancer. I vaguely remember speaking with the anesthesiologist as I slowly transitioned into unconsciousness. I later awakened to a room full of medical professionals. They were all focused on specific tasks including the nurse who was sitting at my side. Apparently, during surgery they attached a plastic bulb to my body for draining purposes. Unfortunately, it was filling up much faster than normal, which meant I was bleeding uncontrollably again. I soon needed to use the rest room and before I knew it, I went unconscious and dropped to the floor.

I could hear my husband and the doctors talking to me, but nothing would come out of my mouth. I felt helpless and afraid. I was taken to the emergency room again where they had to re-open my incisions to find out where the bleeding was coming from. Unfortunately, I was brought back to the room only to be found bleeding again uncontrollably. Once again, I was taken back to the operating room where they again re-opened my incision to get a better understanding of why I was bleeding. After the second time, the doctor realized that an artery had been damaged, which was causing me to bleed. Needless to say, it had been a very tough night. However, this would only be the beginning to my cancer journey. Next came six cycles of chemotherapy and months of recovery.

My cancer journey has taught me many things, but most importantly it has taught me how to cultivate resilience to live longer and fight harder. It has taught me how to look within myself to gain the strength needed to live my best life. Cancer has brought me to my knees on many occasions and because I understood my purpose for living, it has taught me to rise and stand on my feet. Today, I stand more grounded than ever before. Every time I begin to get discouraged by the thought of the re-occurrence of cancer I think of what I have been through. I think of the emotional and physical pain. I think of my mortality and the impact that it would have on my family. Then I realize, I survived then and I am surviving now.

For anyone who is battling cancer, I want you to know that your rise is in proportion to your resourcefulness. Just like effective leaders, you don't have to know all the answers, you just have to know where to find them. Maybe the solution to resilience as you battle cancer isn't necessarily re-connecting with your purpose. It's possible you already have that accomplished. However, maybe you lack the skills to ask for help in times of need. Maybe you can't get out of your own way and it's stopping you from loving you or achieving a breakthrough. Maybe you lack the motivation to find the strength to overcome the unexpected baggage that comes with cancer. Whatever it may be, find the courage to hold on. Sometimes we work so hard to survive without realizing we are, in fact, surviving.

I Still Survive

My spirit bruised my ambitions depleted
My passion for life, I feel robbed and defeated
But through it all, as I fight the tears in my eyes
It's because of a power greater than myself, I still survive

You've rocked my world, you've rained on my parade
You uprooted my anchor you've caused my faith to sway
But through it all, as I prepare to succumb to your demise
As you've shaken me to my core, yet I still survive

You taint my perception of what my future could hold
You keep me in the dark, let the truth be told
But through it all, it's my light that gives me the strength to thrive
Like the homeless in desperation somehow, I still survive

I tiptoe in silence afraid of you being resurrected
Fear you will rise again and chemo or radiation won't protect me
But through it all, faith has proven to save many lives,
Mine is unshakeable, unbreakable, unmistakable, that's why I still survive

You pounce into my life like a leopard claiming its stake
You act as if you own me, and I have nothing to say
As if my self-worth is for sale, and I'm ok with being bribed
You have no idea the value of my worth, that's why I still survive

You have me running in all directions, in disbelief and in awe
Trying to make sense of your intentions, how was I the luck of the draw?
But through it all, I've managed to stay on my feet, and refuse to hide
I hold on to hope like the falsely accused who hungers for freedom, that's
why I still survive

The reality of your existence tries to suffocate my hopes and dreams
It tries to squander my ambitions jeopardizing my self-esteem
But through it all, I live on purpose, I fight to be alive
I'm unapologetic about who I am, that's why I still survive

You try to distort my identity and replace the word victim with my name
But I refuse to give in to your disease stricken ways, I refuse to play your games
Like a treasure chest filled with opulent jewels, I know my worth inside
My value is not dictated by you or anyone else, that's why I still and
will survive

Go With the Flow to Optimize the Best of You

Life, at best, is priceless. It provides a stage for you to fumble and learn the greatest lessons to showcase your skills and talents. Life reveals clues to the paths you should take to live grounded with your purpose. This will allow you to validate your calling and maximize your potential. On the other hand, life wouldn't be life if it didn't contain the essence of unpredictability, requiring you to battle its uncompromising and life altering tendencies, challenging you to question your strength, faith, and purpose. Regardless of the circumstances life brings your way, the more prepared you are the more resilient you become.

Preparing for the unexpected may seem counterintuitive. However, your power lies in your ability to not control the event itself, but rather control your reaction to it. There is a fundamental difference. When these unwanted or spirit-breaking events present themselves, we must focus our time and energy on what we can do to survive the effects they have on our lives. By doing so, it will put you in a position to nurture a performance worthy of praise. Otherwise, they have the potential to consume the very essence of who you are. Therefore, to protect your sanity and livelihood it becomes essential to come to terms with life's endless possibilities, the good and the bad.

With each possibility lies the potential for character building and personal growth. You just have to decide how to make the situation advantageous to you. Also, when that unforeseeable event happens in your life, you want to make sure that you're not so caught off guard that it cripples and destroys you. Such things include: divorce, loss of a job, death of a loved one, financial hardships, failing health, life threatening injuries, victimization, mental breakdowns, and strained relationships. Each offers its own set of challenges. However, the more we can minimize the impact by understanding that this is "life," the less chance the impact has to knock us down. The act of minimizing can begin by asking yourself these relevant and important questions when the unexpected does happen:

- What resources do I have within me and beyond me to thrive during this unexpected event to help me cope in the most resilient way?

- If fear presents itself as a result of this unforeseen circumstance, what is the most productive way to minimize the effects it has on my life?

- What similar experience can I draw from to help me gain the strength and understanding I need to overcome my circumstance?

The act of being knocked down isn't a problem in and of itself. It's only a problem when you don't know how to get back up or you make a subconscious decision not to. In both cases, you are not utilizing

> The act of being knocked down isn't a problem in and of itself. It's only a problem when you don't know how to get back up or you make a subconscious decision not to.

the power within to step up and operate from your highest self. By keeping an open mind and being aware of the resources available to you (yes, you are your own best resource) you are less likely to become a victim of your circumstance. This idea wasn't quite engrained in my consciousness or as fully appreciated by me then as it is today.

The Waves of Life Can Be The Best Teacher

I recently went on vacation to Fort Lauderdale, Florida, where I had an opportunity to swim in the ocean. As I swam, I would find myself periodically taking breaks to take in the moment and enjoy the breathtaking view. Every time I found myself getting lost in my thoughts, a powerful and unexpected wave would come and knock me off my feet. My solution was to bury my feet in the sand as far as they could go, so that when the wave hit me, I would stand less chance of being knocked down. I wanted to win no matter what, but every time I stood up to those powerful and unrelenting waves, regardless of my determination and will to succeed, the force seemed much greater than me. I felt as if I was being tested, but I also knew that if I chose to challenge its formidable and domineering force, I would not win. I also knew that if I kept doing what I was doing, I was going to keep getting what I was getting.

Something had to change and I was smart enough to know that it had to be me. Was it the first time I had been in the ocean? No. Was it the first time I came to the realization of its overbearing power? No. However, each wave that struck my vulnerable and defenseless body brought a sense of familiarity. However, this time something was different. In that moment, it seemed as if I had reached a level of consciousness which I had never experienced before. It was the first time I can remember being intentionally and mentally present in the ocean where I tried to seek a deeper understanding of my experience.

I felt as if I could influence the effects of those waves. Not changing their ability to come into contact with my body, but I would prepare for them when they did. Therefore, instead of standing up to the waves, I decided to jump as they approached me.

I figured I would have greater success and a better outcome if I allowed myself to work with the wave rather than stand against it. It worked; I ultimately decided to go with the flow, both literally and figuratively. As I jumped, I noticed that most of the water appeared to be going around me rather than over me. I didn't feel as if I was being consumed and overtaken by the waves. I felt as if I had some control and a stake in my destiny thus influencing the impact the waves had on my body. I became more empowered one wave at a time and it felt good. Needless to say, if I can do it, so can you!

We Are All Susceptible to "Life"

Remember, the unexpected happens to all of us. It doesn't engage in discriminatory practices. We are all susceptible to its positive and negative influences. It sees no color. It doesn't care about your social or economic status. It doesn't matter if you're in good or poor health, go to church every Sunday, are dedicated to volunteering, refrain from drugs and alcohol, pay your bills on time, or assume the position of a leader or follower, it provides equal opportunities in terms of who it affects. The key is learning to control its effects and understanding the barriers that contribute to your inability to manage it.

There are various reasons as to why you may not be in the best position to manage life's unexpected events. One of the reasons could simply be your age. Maybe you haven't lived long enough to experience many of life's hardships. As a result, when you do encounter them you are ill-prepared to survive them. "Life" hasn't tapped you on the shoulder often enough and made its presence known so that you appreciate it for what it's worth. It hasn't had an opportunity to school you on the "hard knocks of life" and because of this, you lack the emotional maturity and/or the mental toughness to survive. If this is the case, don't worry. Every day has the potential to teach us new lessons. Life has a way of contributing to your growth by way of failed experiences and unexpected events. You just have to be willing to embrace them, the good and the bad, and find the gems that rest among them. They are gems that will allow you to shine as the best version of you. Therefore, regardless of your age, learn to welcome all that life has to offer. Life is the best teacher. It's just a matter of you allowing yourself to become the best student.

Additionally, you may have a tendency to see things as you want rather than seeing things as they really are. If you can't assess your circumstances truthfully without judgement, you're more likely to be critical of life's events. You're more likely to have trouble separating your emotions and expectations from the reality of your unexpected situation. For instance, if you are suddenly in jeopardy of being on the receiving end of a failed or broken relationship due to any number of factors, assess the situation with an open mind. Ask yourself key questions to gain better clarity.

These questions could include, what did I do to contribute to this situation? Am I better off without this person, and if so how? Is this relationship worth fighting for? If so, what actions can I take that are not only good for our relationship, but also my health and well-being? On the other hand, when you don't approach the unexpected with clarity and pass judgement, you minimize your power to thrive in the face of adversity. You are more likely to let your preconceived notions and distorted views that stem from fear taint your reality by being selective in how you manage life's events.

Another reason why you may be detrimentally impacted by the unexpected events in your life is fear. Fear of the unknown has severely impacted the lives of many. When you live in fear and are afraid to face those things in life that could strain you yet also change you, you will never gain the strength necessary to weather the storms of life. Why? When you live in fear of the unexpected you constantly live life with caution. Rather than take chances on your hopes and dreams, you find yourself having reservations about acting in pursuit of them. You find yourself living guarded because you're afraid of what could happen rather than living your life based on what you want to happen.

You see opportunities to grow you and be you, but you don't have the courage to break free of the mental and emotional shackles that are holding you captive. I say, live freely. Trust that life is going to happen no matter what. Trust and know that your fears do not serve you especially in moments of uncertainty. They will cause you to run like a coward. They will make you doubt your capabilities, forcing you to surrender when the going gets tough. When this happens, acknowledge it for what it is. Let that pain that is rooted inside of you be the catalyst for your biggest and boldest breakthrough. The unexpected may surprise you, but never give it enough power to silence you.

Time to Rise and Shine!

- *Understand The True Meaning of Life*
  The reality is we are only on this planet for what seems like a blink of an eye. From the day we are born, nothing is ever promised to us, including good health. Therefore, we must learn to accept what life has to offer, the good, the bad and the ugly. Understand that being in charge of your destiny comes with limitations. We are often told that we can do anything as long as we put our minds to it, and, yes, I believe if you want something in

life, you should make it your mission to accomplish it. However, in the same breath, I am also saying that not every man, woman and child lives to get old. We must come to accept life for what it is and know that things can change with or without our consent at any moment.

I say this to you with love and endearment because I don't want you to lose focus and perspective on what really matters. Steve Jobs once said, "Remembering that I'll be dead soon is the most important tool I've ever encountered to help me make the big choices in life. Because almost everything - all external expectations, all pride, all fear of embarrassment or failure - these things just fall away in the face of death, leaving only what is truly important." I want to inspire you to live fully with intention and power.

I believe we can learn a lot from nature to understand the meaning of life. When you feel as though life no longer serves you in a way that makes you come alive, rather than looking within yourself, look outside of yourself to see the beauty around you. Let the leaves on the ground remind you that you must let go of some things in order to bring about change. Let the snow remind you to slow down and get still to find meaning and purpose. Let the re-growth and budding of plants remind you to regain your strength to live a life of resilience. Let the plush and vibrant flowers that are in full bloom give you the inspiration to live fully. Like nature, you bring life to the world, which means a lot.

• ## Look Back to Get Ahead

Have you ever said to yourself, "How in the world am I going to get through this?" If so, you are not alone. Over the years, I've learned to rely on the strength of my past to help me get through my most difficult circumstances. I've had to consciously reflect on those events that I've overcome to truly understand what it will take to conquer this new challenge in my life. I've had to say to myself, "Well if you've gotten through that, surely you can get through this." I believe by becoming a lifelong learner and committing to self-awareness, you put yourself in a position to learn from the past, but more importantly how you can change your thoughts and actions to have a brighter and more fulfilling future.

I believe some things, particularly those things that we are averse to, show up repeatedly in our lives in different forms to remind us of the importance of learning from our past; meaning if you don't learn from your mistakes you are sure to repeat them. Old situations can present themselves in new ways, and if we are tuned in and aware, we can become strategic and deliberate in looking for the How in our experiences rather than the Why. The 'why' will only get you so far, because it keeps you grounded and focused on the results, but the 'how' will give you the blueprint to look at your circumstance objectively to alter your results, making it more advantageous to your well-being.

To be clear, preventing things such as cancer or any life altering event from happening is not always in your control. However, it is within your power to step up and reflect on those things you have overcome so that it gives you the momentum, willpower, and fortitude to not only survive, but thrive. As you reflect on those past circumstances, ask yourself, "What mindset was I in during that time that gave me the confidence to face my challenges? What type of external support did I have to help me get through my struggles? What factors contributed to me acting in a way that supported my journey to healing and restoration of hope? Bottom line, you want to become a detective in your own life to seek out those things that will make your life bigger and better.

- *Go With the Flow*

  Although life is unpredictable and full of uncertainty, it's important not to let life's events stop you from moving forward to achieving your potential. Living your life in fear serves no one, most importantly, you. Life allows us to experience so many incredible things and even when we are having experiences that are less than desirable, we should see them as gifts in disguise because despite its lack of appeal and your inability to see its value, it still has the potential to change your life even if it's simply your perspective. Why? Because with your new perspective you've stimulated and activated key areas in your brain that have been dormant. It allows your senses to awaken in a new and improved way whether to further your life, or the life of someone else.

  Go with the flow and stop resisting the natural progressions of life. Life is designed to take us places we've never been. It wants to poke and prod you to keep you alive and focused on the things that truly matter. It drives us to awaken or jolt the emotions within us that are needed to thrive and remain hungry for what life has to offer. Your ability to be flexible and go with the flow is directly related to your to your ability to manage and overcome life's unforeseen challenges. When you allow yourself to rise above the tides with open eyes you are able to see a greater distance. You have fewer surprises. Your expectations of what's coming your way are grounded in reality. You're more likely to move with intention and mental agility to dodge some of those overbearing waves of life.

  To rise above the tide and go with the flow, be optimistic. Let hope channel your energy in a direction that will lead you to a path that will replenish your soul and mend your broken spirit. Therefore, when you feel as if resistance has gotten the best of you, take purposeful actions to restore your resilience. Question the validity of your self-doubt, act on your instincts and embrace open-mindedness. This is by no means an exhaustive list; however, it will put you on the right path to not only avoid being consumed by resistance, but to rise in spite of it.

Chapter 10

BELIEVE YOU ARE ENOUGH

When you get to a place where you understand
that love and belonging your worthiness,
is a birthright and not something you have to earn,
anything is possible.
Brene Brown

At a young age, I learned not only the power of words, but even more so the power of a woman's body. The power in her stride, the width of her curvaceous hips, and the thickness of her thighs was a recipe for poetry in motion. Witnessing how women, particularly black women, were revered and praised for their bodily perfections often captivated my impressionable mind. All it took was waiting at the bus stop with my mother and three siblings to fully understand.

My mother was an attractive woman. She seemed to have what many men wanted and it was obvious. Regardless of the season, whenever we took the bus to my grandparent's house it often had a predictable and fortuitous ending. A sleek and often custom-designed Cadillac slowly pulling up to the curb. It was usually as stylish as the man who drove it. He would slowly lean over the passenger seat while remaining calm, cool, and collected to make his presence known. "Hey, you need a ride?" Voice as smooth as butter, a smile as wide as the ocean, and a bravado that was mild enough to feel non-threatening, but bold enough to feel the essence of his manliness was apparently enough to get my mother to say yes. Worrying about safety during that time didn't seem as important as it could be today.

I also witnessed how other women in the community were treated as a result of their physical attributes. A black woman entering a room with all the "right stuff" suddenly turned an ordinary and uneventful day into a spectacle. Although it would appear to be an unconscious choice, both men and women were transfixed by the sway of her hips and her voluptuous backside. Consequently, I would especially notice women who were not as physically endowed go silent as their eyes followed her every move. Men, on the other hand, seemed to have no problem vocalizing their lust or sexual prowess. A whistle, sexually derogatory, or a literal jaw-drop often signified their sentiments.

To be put in a position to command so much power was beyond my comprehension. Yet, I understood that you were either born with those physical attributes or you weren't. Well, apparently, I wasn't and it didn't help that I was constantly reminded of it. High school was an especially difficult time to come to the realization that I was not blessed with "the goods." Or that I wasn't enough. I didn't have what was considered the right stuff, at least that's what was conveyed to me on multiple occasions.

"Michelle you're perfect from the waist up" is what Larry Wilkerson told me in class as he carefully deconstructed and analyzed my body from head to toe. He was tall, dark, not quite handsome, yet his words that imbued confidence made a big impact. I was at a loss for words. My breathing became shallow. My heartbeat, which often went unnoticed, was as loud as the mental chatter that consumed my mind with each beat jolting me into the present moment. Suddenly, seeking a stapler to staple my class assignment became irrelevant and miniscule in scope compared to what I was feeling. I was self-conscious and embarrassed to say the least.

No one had ever been that blunt and openly judgmental about my body. As I stood there trying to digest his words I realized that it was much easier to digest the stinky ole' chitterlings my grandfather would cook than to digest those unpleasant and disheartening words. At least with granddaddy's chitterlings the smell would eventually dissipate and after time leave little traces of its pungency. Whereas Larry's words, unbeknownst to me, would haunt me for years to come.

To make matter worse, two other classmates found the need to categorize me and two other girls based on our body types. The main criteria for determining which category you were in depended on the size of your butt. You would have thought with their careful attention to detail and their serious demeanor, they weren't just high school students, they were qualified to be judges in the Miss America Pageant. After their findings, they somehow concluded that I was in the middle. I don't know which was worse: the fact that I was being compared to other girls or the fact that I was relieved that I wasn't last. Either way, I still felt as if I wasn't enough. Then it came time to go to college.

By the time I arrived in college, I had started wearing clothes that were two sizes too big to compensate for my self-esteem. I thought wearing clothes that were too big would make me look bigger and therefore more acceptable, especially in the black community. I believe I subconsciously wanted to give the impression that I was a bona fide "sista girl." I wanted to genuinely fit in. I wanted them to see me and approve of me as if I was enough.

When I would go and work out in the gym, I wore oversized

sweat shirts and pants. Ironically, I ended up meeting the love of my life there. He later admitted that he didn't realize I had ample breasts because I wore oversized shirts. Whenever we reminisce about those days, we laugh. However, the body image in the black community is so ingrained in our culture of what's acceptable and what isn't that somehow you feel as if you're always being judged.

After going home for a family visit, I decided to visit one of my aunts. This particular day, I wore a new summer dress that I was especially fond of. It was a soft blue and white pin-striped sleeveless dress. It had a lovely belt that I could tie in a bow to accentuate my waist. The bottom of the dress flared out adding a sense of style and sophistication to it. As I approached the front porch where I noticed my aunt sitting, I was consciously aware of the beauty of my dress. She immediately welcomed me home and told me how nice I looked in that dress. She wanted to know where I got it from. I gladly told her.

It was just a matter of time before my excitement would come to a sudden halt. "Lift up your dress and let me see your legs." It was apparent that she wanted to see the size of my legs to determine if whether or not they were acceptable based on her expectations. In response, I lifted the bottom of my dress. As I did, it seemed to slowly bring my sprit down as well as triggered old memories. I wanted to believe that we as a family had evolved beyond that mentality. That our worth was not contingent on our body type, but more so the content of our character.

It's been said that when you know better you do better. I would also like to believe that when you know better you feel better. You feel better about who you are and have a greater appreciation for how you show up in the world. All of which contribute to your self-worth. Fortunately, today I recognize more fully who I am as a person, as black woman in America. I understand the historical weight that has been placed on our shoulders to become human pillars in creating sustainable and healthy families within and beyond the black communities. I understand the societal pressures to conform to white America whether it's the styling of our hair, the way we talk to express our emotions or the way we heal to manage our grief. Even more so, I understand who I was born to be is not limited by how America thinks I should be.

I believe the awareness of my ancestral lineage and the contributions of people of color have helped me to view my worth in a broader context. It's helped me to look beyond self-defeating thoughts and body shaming to accept a more comprehensive view of my worth. My worth extends beyond my narrow hips, the fullness of my lips. It extends beyond the color of my skin and the alopecia on my scalp. It extends beyond the childhood scars on my skinny legs and the scars on my chest as a result of my double mastectomy. My scars no longer represent defects and dysfunction, but rather beauty and acceptance. I am me. I am my own light. I am perfect and so are you.

Take Back Your Power to Love You and Be You

Feeling as though you are enough is essentially operating from an empowered state of mind. It's a state which produces a quality of life that affords you the ability to optimize your life in the most meaningful way. It allows you to accept who you are without the validation of others, or the need for material possessions to dictate your worth. Therefore, you no longer yearn for things outside of yourself to complete you. You complete you.

You give yourself the freedom to live life based on your terms. You have the power to define your beauty, level of intellect, capabilities, and destiny Thus providing you the foundation to live a life of contentment by feeling appreciative for what you have and where you are in the present moment spiritually, physically, and mentally. It's only when you allow yourself to rise to this level of being that you can truly feel as if you are rising up to shine out in the world and deliver your best performance.

As I've traveled my path in life, I've had the opportunity to witness manifestations of self-worth and how they've impacted the performances of others. It comes as no surprise when I see someone embracing their humanity and thus living beyond the limitations of the world. A world that, if you are not careful, will reel you in like a fish fighting for dear life as it succumbs to a slow and powerless death.

Those who manage to survive and rise above the tides are able to see beyond the horizon to realize their potential. They seem to have an endless stream of self-knowing. They appear to have a firm understanding of who they are and are not easily swayed by the opinions and judgements of others. Why? Their self-perception is grounded in truth and is a reflection of their values, which reign higher than any external sources outside themselves.

People who embrace themselves fully see beyond the superficial measures or standards of living to search for more meaning and depth as it relates to their self-worth. As a result, they perform with greater confidence, develop an affinity for resilience, and have the tendency to attract positive people, places, and things in their lives. It's as if they are resolute in the definition of who they are and what they stand for. It's a definition they've created as a measuring stick to guide their principles and uphold their values. Furthermore, when anyone or anything appears to jeopardize their truth or convictions they have the internal fortitude or bandwidth to bear its weight. Needless to say, they are often stronger than they appear because their strength is derived not from their physical state of being but rather their internal state of being.

- From what sources do you derive your self-worth?
- Are you channeling your energy and mindset in a way that serves you?

- What will it take for you to elevate your self-worth in order to live unchained by other people's misguided judgements?

No matter the answer, what we do know is that your ability to protect and preserve your self-worth is a goal worthy of putting in the effort to accomplish. On the other hand, those who struggle to accept themselves as enough and fail to deliver their optimum performance tend to fall on the other end of the spectrum. They tend to believe those who achieve any type of success worthy of praise were born with special gifts and talents. They believe they were overlooked and are undeserving of notable skills and capabilities. They believe that someone else holds the key to their success and to attain it, one must rely on others. Although they may see what's possible through the actions of others, it somehow seems out of reach. Consequently, their vision for success soon perishes and becomes a figment of their imagination.

Those who struggle have self-talk that is often rooted in negativity and further demonstrates their narrow views of who they are and the value they add to those around them. It's often a choice of words that slowly erodes the human spirit and leaves behind the remains of unfulfilled hopes and dreams. It is words that undermine their creativity and imagination to see what's possible due to their inability to realize their human potential. As for the choices they make, they are often rooted in fear because they want to play it safe without recognizing the need to move beyond their comfort zone.

Small Minded Thoughts Produce Small Minded Actions

Becoming complacent in your comfort zone further perpetuates insecurity causing you to adopt the belief that you are not worthy or deserving of your desires. I must remind you, you are worthy and even more so, you are enough. Don't let your small-minded thoughts of feeling as though you are not enough create small-minded actions. Give your actions purpose so that they are driven by intentionality. Let them be proportionate to and in alignment with your thoughts and aspirations.

There is a reason why it's been said that actions speak louder than words. This is why self-awareness and the management of your thoughts is key. Let the truth be told: your actions are a reflection of your thoughts. If you think on a level that is beneath your innate ability to stand in your power and perform at your best, it is inevitable that you will shortchange your self-worth. You will rob the very essence of who you think you are, but more importantly, who you have the potential to become.

The truth is you are the quintessential embodiment of greatness with the ability to transcend from your darkest moments to the highest levels of enlightenment. Your ability to rise and withstand life's turbulent and unpredictable ways is inherently engrained in the essence of your true nature. Therefore, let your worth shower the universe with the riches of your humanity. Let the core of who you are pour out upon yourself and others until it fills every crevice of your soul. Let your authentic self rise up to live a life of freedom, fuel your aspirations and ability to experience your optimum performances.

How can you expect to seek a higher calling and obtain the fruits of your labor when you diminish your worth and rob yourself of the

> Your ability to rise and withstand life's turbulent and unpredictable ways is inherently engrained in the essence of your true nature. Therefore, let your worth shower the universe with the riches of your humanity.

ability to see what's possible? It would be impossible. Therefore, the sooner you come to the realization of who you truly are and what you bring to the world, the sooner you learn to identify with the greatness that lies within you. A greatness that is then built on a solid foundation. Needless to say, you were created to carry a weight much greater than yourself. When the load gets heavy and you feel as though life is too great to bear, and you feel yourself caving in, know that your inner strength can only be accessible by first believing what's possible. By appreciating the skills, gifts and resources that you innately have, it will give you the inspiration to believing what's possible, but even more so, that you are enough.

Empowered Voices Change Lives

There is a young woman by the name of Greta Thunberg. She embodies the idea of what it means to value and embrace your self-worth. Greta is a young environmental activist for climate change. She was a speaker at the 2019 Climate Action Summit where she had an opportunity to speak to world leaders about the impact of climate change and their role in combating this issue. I was moved by her speech for a number of reasons, but it was her presence and her ability to recognize her worth that made her speech most captivating and worthy of praise.

Whether you buy into her position regarding this topic is not the issue. By reducing the speech simply to the topic, you would trivialize a momentous event that at the very least deserves to be seen for what it's worth. You don't have to agree with her philosophy or political agenda to take notice of her voice and how she uses it to demonstrate not only the value of her words but also the value of who she is as a person.

When asked, "What's your message to world leaders today?"

Greta responded by saying, "My message is, we'll be watching you." The words to follow are just as powerful, if not more so. "This is all wrong I shouldn't be up here. I should be back in school on the other side of the ocean. Yet, you all come to young people for hope. How dare you. You have stolen my dreams and childhood with your empty words. Yet I am one of the lucky ones. People are suffering." To say these words with such passion and conviction takes tenacity and courage. It takes a self-knowing that seems to be beyond her years on this planet. Yet she sits with composure while displaying an assertive posture that exudes self-confidence. Speaks with a voice that is soft in tone, yet jolting enough to get the attention of world leaders. She appears unapologetic in her delivery as she highlights their lack of consideration and the repercussions of their actions or lack thereof.

It is clear that she has an objective, which is to get world leaders to listen to and heed her message. Needless to say, every word that comes out of her mouth supports that objective. Why? Because she knows what she stands for and what's at stake. She allows herself to rise up and shine while delivering an authentic performance. A performance that appears to be so grounded in her truth that any actor of any significance would aspire to achieve.

As a child, I can't say that I always had confidence like Greta to believe that I was enough. I couldn't see the riches of my character, the value of my words, or the beauty within and outside of myself. It took years of self-reflection and the opportunity to tell my story through poetry to fully understand that I was enough.

Time to Rise and Shine!

• *Appreciate Who You Are Today*

Learn to appreciate who you are now more so than who you aspire to be in the future. Go out of your way to find the gems that are hidden within you and outside of you. Let those gems serve to optimize you and elevate your self-esteem so that you can have a greater appreciation for who you are. When you validate who you are, you communicate to yourself that where you are in life is where you deserve to be based on your previous decisions. You don't live in regret. You don't look back and say, "I should be further in life because… or "I should have more to show for what I have been through." The reality is you are where you are and who you are because of your past experiences and the actions you've taken as a result of them.

Accept and own the idea that you are responsible for creating you and if you don't like the piece of work that you have constructed, it's time to rebuild you, starting with a solid foundation. It's a foundation that is created with the mindset of knowing that you are enough. One of the things you can do to elevate your self-worth is to avoid mind-reading. Mindreading causes you to jump to conclusions that are not only inaccurate, but self-destructive.

To avoid mindreading be proactive in retrieving the correct information rather than speculating what others may be thinking. This can be achieved by asking the right questions. Examples include, "What did you think of my performance?" "Do you think I am skilled enough to move on to the next level? If not, in your opinion, what were my strengths and weaknesses? What do you think I could have done differently to exceed your expectations?" In addition, to appreciate who you are today learn to stop minimizing your accomplishments. Allow yourself the opportunity to discover your gifts and talents by accepting them wholeheartedly. Let the world see all that you have to offer. Playing small will not serve you, but playing big in the world will ultimately transform you.

- ### *Live According to Your Values*
  Values are strongly held beliefs that inform you how to live your life. They shape and guide you by creating boundaries and expectations on which to base your life. They help you to create meaning and to fulfill your purpose with authenticity. When you honor your values and believe that you are enough because of them, you walk through the world differently. Your walk signifies your inner strength because you know who you are and where you stand.

  When you live according to your values, in essence, you're living according to your truth. Since your values are a representation of your beliefs and if you act upon those beliefs, how you show up in the world will become a true reflection of you. Consequently, who you really are will always be more than enough. This concept is so powerful, yet so true.

  You live according to your values by first identifying what they are. If you have difficulty trying to identify them simply ask yourself these questions. "What am I willing to die for? What thoughts keep me up at night? When was the last time I cried and why? What beliefs do I hold near and dear to my heart? What stories do I hear that evoke passion and empathy?" These are just a few examples and they are quite revealing if you answer them honestly and with depth. Once you have a clear understanding of what your values are, honor them by making them a part of your daily life. As a result, your self-worth will inevitably increase because your life isn't based on trends or superficial ideals. It is based on you seeing yourself for who you really are and giving yourself permission to love you and be you.

- ### Develop Self-Compassion

  We as a people are generally not taught how to be self-compassionate. The more self-compassionate we are the more we run the risk of being viewed as someone who is self-indulgent. However, when we find it within ourselves to forgive our mistakes and understand what we are going through, we create a sense of inner peace and contentment. In addition, the act of self-compassion has a way of nurturing your soul by opening your heart to let you in.

  We let other people in our heart, but do we always let ourselves in our heart? Unfortunately, we don't. Yet, when you do let yourself in you build trust within yourself because when you engage in self-compassion you are not relying on anyone to approve or disapprove of you. You control your destiny. John O'Donohue once said, "When you are compassionate with yourself you trust your soul which you let guide your life. Your soul knows the geography of your destiny better than you do." Therefore, being compassionate with yourself will lead you to a healthier, more resilient physical and emotional well-being.

  You can begin to show yourself compassion and cultivate self-worth through writing. There have been numerous studies on the benefits of self-compassion writing. Being that we all, at some point in our lives, have said and done things that we are not proud of, this would be a good place to start. For instance, Dr. Kristin Neff, Associate Professor, Educational Psychology Dept., University of Texas at Austin suggests it would be beneficial to write about your imperfections. "Try writing about an issue you have that tends to make you feel inadequate or bad about yourself (physical appearance, work or relationship issues). What emotions come up for you when you think about this aspect of yourself? Try to feel your emotions exactly as they are-no more no less- and then write about them. In addition, she suggests, "Write a letter to yourself from the perspective of an unconditionally loving imaginary friend." Ideally, you want this friend to be loving, kind, and understanding. They recognize your strengths and your weaknesses, but most importantly, they recognize that you are human. As you're writing from their perspective be transparent and honest, but also gentle and compassionate. Be good to yourself. You are worth it!

Chapter 11

REDEFINE YOUR SELF-WORTH

*I have learned that as long as I hold fast to my beliefs and values
—and follow my own moral compass—
then the only expectations I need to live up to are my own.*
Michelle Obama

addy Mae, she sure was something. She was a fictitious character I created in my play, "Elma Gene's Journey's To Freedom" based on the 1963 Children's Crusade in Birmingham Alabama. She was a determined and zestful child who fought for her civil rights and the rights of others. Early on, she learned that her self-worth was non-negotiable and because of her unrelenting faith and commitment to the struggle, she proved it wasn't. In the play, she makes the mistake of trying on a dress in a clothing store. This was a big no-no considering she was a person of color during a time of racial segregation.

The scene goes as follows, "Mama can Charlotte and I go in that store right there? No mama, that one! The one with the pretty dresses in the window. Please, pretty please." Her mother obviously affirms her wishes. "Thank you mama. Come on Charlotte! Charlotte doesn't that look like the dress that Darla wore in that Little Rascals movie?

I sure do wish I could try it on. Look, I have an idea." Haddy begins to whisper in Charlotte's ear.

She cautiously looks around to make sure she is not being watched. When she feels safe to do so, she quickly attempts to try on a dress. "Wow, I love it. It's so fluffy and soft, I could just eat it up." Suddenly Haddy gasps for air. The store attendant forcefully pulls her by the ear. "Ouch! Ouch! I'm sorry. I just wanted to try it on, that's all. I didn't mean no harm, I promise. Ma'am, please don't call the police. I don't want to go to jail, Mama!"

The older and present day Haddy Mae begins to reflect on that moment. "That was the first time I felt as if being colored was like being dirty. That night, I went home and took a long bath. I remember thinking if I could be white like those white folks, then I could go back in that store and try on that dress. So, I soaped up my washcloth real good and I scrubbed and scrubbed my body. I so wanted to get all the color off so that I could be white, but the more I scrubbed the redder my skin got, and before I knew it, my skin started to bleed. When I realized the color wasn't gonna come off, I just sat there and cried."

I find it rather interesting that although Haddy was a fictitious character, the aftermath of her experience with racial injustice is still relevant today. An experience that forces you to question your self-worth and your ability to rise beyond adversity to become a resilient human being. As a young adult, I questioned if Haddy Mae and I were one and the same, but what I do know is just like Haddy Mae, my experience had as deep and profound effect on my life.

It was just an ordinary day, or so I thought. After parking my car in the parking lot as I had done on various occasions, I gathered my belongings to head into the school building. I was feeling confident and self-assured as I was there to complete some additional training to fulfill my student teaching obligations. My attire was professional.

My demeanor was amiable and I wanted nothing more than to be the best teacher I could be. I was proud of the person I was becoming.

My self-worth seemed to grow exponentially with every sign that I was doing a great job and that day I had no reason to believe otherwise. Being that I had visited this particular school on previous occasions as a student teacher without any unusual encounters taking place, I just assumed my day would end as expected. Unfortunately, I soon discovered that this was the furthest from the truth. Little did I know, my self-worth would be challenged as my vulnerabilities would be on display for students to witness.

As I entered the building, a familiar looking white woman who appeared to be a security guard or hall monitor for some reason responded as if she had never seen me before. Without a logical explanation, she decided to physically search me. I couldn't believe what was happening. I was confused and embarrassed to say the least. In retrospect, I felt as if Haddy Mae and I were one and the same. Just as she had been robbed of her dignity and respect so had I. I felt as if I wanted to be rescued, but there was no one who could save me. Needless to say, my world felt very small at that moment.

I instinctively complied with her intrusive and unwelcoming actions. I regrettably downplayed my assertiveness only to compromise my self-worth and integrity. The moment I looked up to regain my composure not only did my world seem smaller, but it was now different. The lens through which I viewed humanity had become blurred and distrusting. I knew the world could be capable of such acts. I knew the world could be vile, disheartening, and cruel. History and the lives of my ancestors would without a doubt confirm my sentiments. However, when you are the one directly impacted by social injustice, it has a way of opening your eyes, breaking your heart, and dimming the light that illuminates your spirit.

I remember telling the teacher I was assigned to work with what had happened. I could tell this type of behavior was unacceptable and that it went against her values. She seemed to listen to me not only with her ears, but with her whole being. Her attentiveness was especially timely since she appeared to be of European descent. I could feel that her energy was attuned with mine. She made me feel emotionally safe to share my story. It should not have been a surprise that she, unknowingly to me, decided to tell the principal what had happened.

I later received a phone call from the principal asking me about the incident. He wanted to know if I felt as if I had been racially discriminated against. I remember telling him no. I wanted to give her the benefit of the doubt. I wanted to believe that she really didn't recognize me and that she was simply doing her job. However, I left that day feeling perplexed and broken. I was perplexed primarily because there have been times when I have reflected on that moment and wondered if I was actually being racially discriminated against because of the color of my skin.

I decided not to tell my supervising teacher, the one who I worked under at my home school, what had happened. I believe subconsciously I wanted those discomfiting feelings and thoughts to disappear. I thought if I no longer talked about what had happened, in some way it would make me feel better. Was it worth it? No. However, now that I am older and wiser, I now have more of an appreciation for my voice and its value.

My eyes witnessed something that day that could have left me broken, but it didn't. I refused to let that moment define me. I was determined to rise above it by holding on to my dignity and embracing my worth as a young black woman. It taught me how I could potentially be seen as a black woman and that my worth hinged on the color of my skin rather than the content of my character. Yes, I know the battles people of color have fought and continue to fight, but that day it was about me. If her motives were racially motivated that means she didn't see me for who I was. She saw only the color of my skin which was enough to tell her the beginning, middle, and end of my story. The good news is, my story is still being written because I am still alive and loving the skin I'm in.

Love the Skin You're in Because You Matter

Part of the challenge of being human is recognizing and embracing the humanity in others. It's a challenge not because we are born lacking the ability to demonstrate compassion for one another, but because over time we become influenced by external factors. These factors include cultural biases, family customs and racial prejudices, which then impact our views of how we value and accept other human beings. The repercussions of these characteristics not only shape how we perceive others, but how they have the ability to profoundly affect our self-worth.

I define self-worth as the value one places on one's self that can either hinder your well-being or empower it by embracing the essence of who you are and not who you aspire to be. When you embrace who you are and find value in the weakest and the most vulnerable parts of your humanity that is grounded in the here and now, your self-worth becomes priceless.

I believe if you can develop an appreciation for the things that you can't change or buy, nothing can rob you of your joy or the compassion you have for yourself. It's because you're not coming from

> When you embrace who you are and find value in the weakest and the most vulnerable parts of your humanity that is grounded in the here and now, your self-worth becomes priceless.

a place of lack, but rather a place of abundance. You find value not only in the things that appear outside of you, but more importantly, the things that are within you.

You Have the Power to Re-Write Your Story

Sometimes we have to redefine how we value ourselves. We have to scrutinize and question our beliefs about who we are and the stories we tell ourselves. The interesting part about telling ourselves stories which often have the potential to define us and destroy us is we are not the sole authors. Our stories are shaped by various institutions. Whether it's a family, religious, or social institution, they all have an effect on how we perceive ourselves, which ultimately determines our self-worth.

As an African American woman, I've had to come to terms with my self-worth on various occasions. I've had to break down the internal walls of self-deprecation. Confront insensitive remarks that had begun to outweigh my true sense of self. I felt as if I had to dig deep to find the core of who I was so that I could own my power and re-connect with my self-worth.

Over time, I've learned that if you neglect to redefine your self-worth and come to terms with the impact it may have on your life, it could result in unfavorable consequences, such as feelings of shame. According to Amber. J. Johnson, "Shame is internalized when shame experiences become part of individual identity (Cook, 1988). Thus, racism can provoke shame responses that are dominant, internalized, and pervasive for African Americans." It's for this reason why it may be difficult for African American women who struggle to find their self-worth to find their voice and express it in an assertive manner. It was also noted that, "Experiences of racism, infused within the constructs of American society, become components of African American Identity. Examples of such permeations include, African

American women's struggle to restrain their emotions for fear of being portrayed as the "Angry Black Woman." Therefore, at times, it may seem easier to internalize the pain rather than address it.

It's much easier to get disillusioned into adopting an altruistic view of the world. You want to believe that we live in a world where people will have to pay the consequences for their actions not based on the color of their skin, but rather the nature of their crimes. A world where you desperately want to give people the benefit of the doubt. You want to believe that they are having a bad day rather than stuck in an unforgiving mindset that lacks compassion and sincerity. You want to believe that people seek to judge one another based on their character and the ability their character has to advance and enrich the lives of others. However, this is not always reality.

We All Have Infinite Value

The reality is there are people who lack the emotional intelligence needed to embrace and understand others' lived experiences and daily struggles. They fail to see how the impact of their actions de-humanize and debilitate others only to advance their own agendas and satisfy their personal needs. Therefore, they have a tendency to look through you rather than at you. As a result, they see a fraction of who you really are. It's as if the part that they do see satisfies their curiosity enough to define you and decline you. What they don't know is the value of their judgements will always be of less value than your true worth. It's for this reason why your self-worth should be based on things that are put into context. If you don't, you will let the world minimize you and cause you to develop an "irrational concept of worth."

The reality is we are all valued differently based on our profession, accomplishments, and cultural backgrounds. Unfortunately, when we don't seem to hit the mark or don't measure up to societal standards, we seem to fall short on the rungs of life. We somehow get categorized as someone who lacks promise or value, but let the truth be told that we all have value. It's the cognitive distortions that stem from society's social and racial inequities that seem to plague our self-perceptions and undermine who we really are. They prevent us from channeling our energy in a direction that nourishes our soul and enhances our self-worth. Therefore, I ask:

- What cognitive distortions are you telling yourself that prohibit you from embracing your self-worth?

- How can you re-define your self-worth to elevate your confidence to breed self-compassion?

- What was the catalyst for your most pressing cognitive distortions? And why did you accept them as truths?

These cognitive distortions present a false reality and are liable to show up in different ways. For instance, Matthew McKay and Patrick Fanning, authors of *Self Esteem*, have identified various ways in which we distort our perceptions that could potentially affect our self-esteem and diminish our self-worth. For instance, overgeneralizations, polarized thinking, and personalization can and will take a toll on your self-worth because they are not grounded in truth. They are based on your emotions rather than logic. Emotions are a response to your thoughts and because our thoughts don't always tell us the truth we don't always see the truth. Unfortunately, this is what causes us to relent to the following cognitive distortions.

Overgeneralization relates to singling out specific people, places, and things and letting them define other people, places, and things in your life. It's having a limited view of the world which taints your ability to see beyond certain things in your life. It keeps you stuck mentally by not embracing other possibilities or gaining alternative perspectives. As a result, your self-worth is compromised because what you don't know will always impact areas in your life in which you will not grow. I will illustrate this example by sharing a story as it relates to a random act of kindness.

My daughter and I went to a local restaurant for lunch. It wasn't until after I ordered my food that I saw a sign at the register to let me know that they were not accepting cash, but they were accepting credit cards. Well, I didn't have my credit card, but I did have $40.00 in cash to pay toward my $23.00 bill. I asked the cashier if she could take cash anyway and she told me that it wasn't possible. I then asked if she could go and get her manager. Well, her manager was in close proximity and told me that they couldn't accept my cash due to some form of technical difficulty. I was a bit frustrated, I mean who doesn't accept cash, right? But I understood. The next thing I knew, the white lady behind me, without hesitation said, "Oh, I'll pay for her food. Just put it on my credit card with the rest of my bill." What? I then said to the lady, "Thank you so much, but here I can give you my cash." She said, "No." I said, "I appreciate you, but why would you do this?" She politely yet firmly said, "Because I can."

My 10-year old daughter and I both said thank you. Then I realized I had something other than cash that she may have found to be of value. I said, "I just created my second poetry CD for cancer survivors, do you know of anyone who has cancer that you may want to share it with? She said, "My friend was just diagnosed with cancer." I then went to my car to get a copy of my CD and a brochure. When I came back to give it to her, the expression on her face reminded me of the expression on my face when she offered to pay for my food-perplexed and appreciative. I would like to believe that there was a special moment shared between the two of us that will impact us well beyond that encounter. I told her I was hungry and she told me she was hangry and we both laughed.

Imagine if I would have let my experience with the school hall-way monitor dictate my perception of white women. Imagine if I wouldn't have allowed myself to be vulnerable by accepting her offer all because I was stuck in the past and allowed my distorted views to influence that moment? Not only would I have missed an opportunity to eat lunch at the restaurant with my daughter, I would have missed out on something much bigger-an opportunity to make a human connection.

Your Thoughts Impact Your Self-Worth

Polarized thinking is also another distortion that has the ability to erode your self-worth. It relates to using definitive terms which rob people or things of their individuality. It doesn't allow you to see the full spectrum of possibilities. You are reduced to having an either or mentality. This way of thinking does not serve you. It cultivates a fixed mindset causing you to lack skills in open mindedness. It forces you to see things head on without taking into account things that lie in your peripheral vision. Just like driving a car, if you don't take into account drivers who may appear on the left of you or the right of you, you could potentially change the course of your life for the worse. Therefore, I want to encourage you to see life through a lens that is bigger and wider than you. This way, your self-worth has a chance to grow in so many areas of your life.

Personalization leads you to believe everything is about you. You are unable to separate yourself from things that are truly not for you or about you. In such cases, you put yourself in a position that promotes feelings of victimization and a sense of hopelessness. Unfortunately, you are rewarded by having a greater propensity towards negative thinking, which compromises your self-worth. The truth is, everything isn't about you. According to Daniel Amen, a psychiatrist and brain disorder specialist known for creating the 18-40-60 rule, "At age 18 people care very much about what others think of them. By age 40, they learn not to worry what others think. By age 60, they figure out that no one was thinking about them in the first place." Therefore, approach feedback and other people's views and opinions objectively. Yes, there will be times when you will be part of the equation, but if you always make things about you, you will always come up short.

Time to Rise and Shine!

- *Pay Attention to the Stories You Tell*
  The stories you tell yourself have a significant impact on how you perceive your self-worth. If you are constantly telling yourself what you can't do or who you can't be, you are less likely to realize your potential. You're less likely to find value in who you are as a person. Choose stories that uplift and inspire you. Let them cause you to come alive and thrive in the midst of your fears so that you can rise and shine in spite of them.

  When you become present and realize that your stories are no longer serving you, simply create a new one by re-framing your narrative. This can be achieved by focusing on what you have rather than what you don't, seeing the upside to things that have the potential to turn your world upside down and showing gratitude for the simplicities in life. It starts with minimizing self-limiting language that ultimately create those stories and can cause you to buy into unfounded beliefs. Therefore, let the words you choose be the building block for the foundation needed to create stories with a lasting and more influential impact.

- *Love You No Matter What*

  Make it a priority to love yourself. So often, we are taught to love other people, but we are rarely taught to love ourselves. Learning to love yourself is a skillset like many others. It requires you to suspend judgement about who you are and accept yourself. It requires you to listen to your inner voice to understand your thoughts and feelings on a much deeper level. You learn to have an appreciation for your truth, which is where you find your value and the real you.

  Loving you no matter what means making time for you. It's scheduling you into your day so that you can have some "me time." It's a time to gather your thoughts, clear your head, contemplate decisions, and replenish your energy. It's what contributes to the optimization of your self-worth. Regardless of which actions you choose to take, ultimately it's about taking control of your health and well-being by making yourself a priority. Loving you means you are not playing the role of the referee in your life, where you are constantly supporting others in their wins and advocating on their behalf. Rather, it's your ability to play on a team in the game of life so that you put yourself in a position to win. So that you are cheering you on to live your best life by increasing your self-worth.

- *Capitalize On Your Strengths*

  Do you know where your strengths lie? Do you know which things you do that allow you to shine and be seen in your best light? If you don't take inventory of your gifts and talents to understand how they serve you and the world, you will not have true perspective of your worth. Therefore, make a concerted effort to own and act on your strengths. Look for clues within you and beyond you by listening to your voice and the trusted voices of others. They will lead you in the right direction and inform you of your most valuable assets as a person.

The clues will be discovered in the response others give you. Responses such as, "I wish I could do that, you make it look so easy, where did you learn that or can you teach me how to do that?" are all signs that whatever you are doing is of value to someone. Consequently, when others recognize your value it increases your self-worth. It has a way of heightening your self-esteem resulting in you feeling good about yourself. It has a way of opening your eyes to seeing other aspects of your humanity.

If you allow yourself to reflect on your wins in life, and not just your losses, you will be in a better position to connect the dots. Sometimes that's the only thing that is stopping you from becoming the person you aspire to be or do the things you want to do. Connect the dots by asking yourself, what do I do best and how can I make the most of it? Or, what are the things I do that cause my spirit to rise when I feel discouraged or helpless? Find it within you to illuminate your strengths. Bring them to the forefront of your consciousness so that you can let your light shine brighter beyond measure.

Chapter 12

"YES, AND" TO ROCK
THE STAGE OF LIFE

If it's a good idea go ahead and do it.
It's much easier to apologize
than it is to ask for permission.
Grace Hopper

L ife, if you're willing and patient, will often put you where you're
supposed to be. It will also show you what is possible if only you
agree to accept the greatness it has to offer. I truly believe that
when life's greatest and most impactful lessons are rejected whether
consciously or not, the window of opportunity could potentially
close indefinitely. However, if you welcome new opportunities, and
are able to challenge and re-define your fears the stage of life affords
you the chance to shine in more ways than one; and that's exactly
what I did.

It's 2018 and I enthusiastically and without hesitation made
the decision to go to TeamWomen's holiday party. TeamWomen is
an organization created to empower women to rise and shine and
achieve their potential. Although I had heard about them on many
occasions, I felt this was the right time to show up, but more importantly to be part of something much bigger than myself.

I was beyond excited, yet didn't know if it would turn out to be a "typical" networking event where people would want to know what you do before they get a chance to know who you are. It's as if they hunger for the need to instinctively put you into a category to satisfy their curiosity and possibly their ego. I didn't want any part of it, yet I prepared my "What I Do" speech just in case. Who am I kidding? I did want people to know what I did and who I helped. I wanted them to appreciate my value so that I could build meaningful relationships, tell my story, and grow my business.

Little did I know, telling my story in this context would be the catalyst for experiencing a life-altering opportunity. An opportunity that would not only strengthen my speaking and performance abilities, but enhance my self-esteem, which was priceless. Soon after I arrived, it was time for the program to begin. I felt confident yet I had a tinge of nervousness being that I arrived alone and didn't anticipate encountering anyone I knew.

I searched for an open seat as I looked to my left and then to my right, but to no avail; it appeared as if I was out of luck. Then, as I looked straight ahead to the front of the room, I spotted an empty table. Within a matter of seconds, it seemed as if I had an overwhelming amount of questions and thoughts running through my mind as I cautiously made my way to the front of the room. "Do I dare sit in the front row? Who do I think I am? Michelle, you sure do have a lot of nerve. You're going to look like a fool sitting at the table by yourself." As the saying goes, I felt the fear and did it anyway. Needless to say, my pathological critics were starting to get the best of me.

It was just a matter of seconds before I was joined by another party-goer. She was physically attractive, but what made her most attractive was her personality and warm smile. We immediately struck up a conversation. I soon felt as if she was someone I had known for a long time. She seemed genuine and down to earth. I liked her; her style, her professionalism and her willingness to be curious about who I was and what I do. How exciting! This is what I had prepared for, right? Wrong. Our conversation went well beyond my "What I Do" statement.

Due to her warm spirit, I unconsciously shared more than I had planned. I told her about me being diagnosed with breast cancer and how I was now on the path to re-building my speaking business. I told her about my military background and other significant accomplishments in my life. The next thing I knew, she called over the Executive Director for me to meet. She told her that she needed to hear my story. From that moment on, I would have never guessed where that introduction would lead me.

A few months after that encounter and after getting to know the Executive Director, who was a kind, warm hearted and impactful leader, my phone rang. It was the Executive Director of TeamWomen. She asked, "Michelle, would you be interested in being the CEO Moderator for our TeamWomen Conference?" I was speechless. Once again, I had those self-limiting thoughts running through my mind as she waited patiently for a response.

I couldn't answer her right away because of course, I was too busy talking to myself. "Are you kidding me? You want me to be the CEO Moderator for your annual conference? No way…really?" Then it dawned on me, I should probably end this conversation with myself so that I could continue the conversation with her—duh!

Once I caught my breath and fully acknowledged her invitation, I anxiously accepted. When I hung up the phone I was overjoyed with excitement. Then reality began to set in and I knew I had work to do to ensure that I was prepared and I was, but you couldn't tell my nerves that the day of the conference.

I was terrified. I couldn't breathe. I felt as if my body was betraying me and I wanted to run as far as my thin and unstable legs can take me. Run into the arms of my maternal grandmother. A woman who once kept me safe from the tumultuous angst of the world. Who tried to wipe every tear that streamed down my narrow face, and who would be willing to fight any battle that posed a threat to my body or anything else. However, as I stood in a sea of 600 people, she was nowhere to be found.

Unfamiliar with my surroundings and those who occupied it, I would periodically run to the stalls of the hotel bathroom to collect my thoughts and my breath; searching for peace and a safe haven to let go and dispose of my fears. If I could have flushed them away, I would have. At that moment, the bathroom stall felt as if it was my saving grace.

I temporarily felt protected and out of harm's way. I guess you can say, in many ways that stall felt like my grandmother's house. Small, yet big enough to meet my needs, but most importantly, it created a barrier from the outside world. A world that would soon be waiting for me to perform and rock the stage, both literally and figuratively.

As I occupied the bathroom, I frantically looked over my tedious notes as I tried to desperately hold on to my self-confidence. I felt prepared. I truly believed I was, but I was embarking on new territory; I was asked to do something that I had never done before, at least not to that level in front of 600 people. I was asked to be the CEO moderator for TeamWomen's Annual Conference for goodness sake!

It was a privilege and honor, but my nerves seemed to overshadow my appreciation and gratitude at that particular moment. Before, I knew it, it was show time. It was time for me to rock the stage. I remember standing in the back of the jam-packed ballroom being assisted with setting up my lapel microphone. The closer the time came for me to recite my poem and moderate the CEO panel, my energy became overwhelming. As I glanced across the room and noticed the amount of people who occupied the space, I immediately thought about the comedian and actor Steve Harvey. In his book *Jump*, he talks about the importance of jumping, which simply means allowing yourself to take risks in pursuit of your dreams and goals. He says, "I have no fears greater than my dreams. Acknowledge your fear and move forward. Fear is there to let you know that what you are taking on is worth risking your current lifestyle. Once you jump, God will take it from there." After these profound and impactful words ran through my mind, I could feel my energy shift. The energy that previously tried to consume me and potentially sabotage my ability to shine was no longer robbing me of my power. I suddenly felt in control and was overtaken by confidence.

As the first words came out of my mouth I said them with intention and power. I began to recite my poem as I weaved through the audience connecting with guests as I looked them in the eye. As I made my way to the stage, those few moments felt surreal, even magical. Now that I look back at that special moment, I realized how far I had come. The thought of feeling interrogated by my mother regarding the five dollars I took, being asked questions by my father's girlfriend about what he had done to me, questioning my grandmother's motives for volunteering and questioning God for why my mother and I had cancer, was now put in perspective.

As I took to the stage moments before conducting the interview, I realized that I was now in a position to not answer questions, but to ask them. They were questions that I was able to ask to some of the most powerful, intelligent and impactful leaders on this planet. The best part of all, just as I was there to support and honor women rising, I realized so was I. I am a woman rising!

Similar to public speaking or acting, reciting poetry is the one time I feel as if I am one with my audience. As if we have an unbreakable bond and I am holding them captive with words of empowerment and inspiration. Once I made it to the stage and joined the CEOs who were waiting for my arrival to conduct the panel interview, I felt as if I was shining and owning the stage. I was prepared, focused, and in the moment.

I See Women Rising
Poem

Intro: When I look into the audience, I don't see you and you and you. I see a collective group of women, who are changing the scope and dynamics of womanhood. Women who are embracing their vulnerabilities, imaginations and creativity by elevating the consciousness and esteem of others through their goods and services. I see women who are uplifting one another to become their potential by expanding their horizons, enabling them to want more, be more, and do more, but even more so…

I see women rising like the warm buttermilk biscuits my grandmamma used to make. Like the golden sun as it rises from the east shining on my black ebony face. Like children as they awaken eagerly and enthusiastically for gifts on a cold Christmas Day; rising hungry, heart pounding, feet stomping, voices screaming, arms hugging as they get lost in the midst of something much greater than themselves.

I see women rising women who are no longer bound by their self-limiting thoughts, fears and insecurities, who are making a difference within and beyond their thriving or impoverished communities. Women who are taking a stand to embrace the light and gifts from within, living beyond the world's expectations and boxes they try to put them in. Fighting for every width and depth of their dreams, creating holes in that box to make fit for a queen.

I see women rising echoing the sentiments and bravery of their ancestors, standing on the shoulders of those who came before them as they pave the way for their successors, wanting more out of life and all things it has in store, yet trying to do better than the generations before, overcoming struggles and obstacles knocking down doors unwilling to compromise their truth to be so much more.

I see women rising like the redwoods and giant sequoias of the ever commanding presence of the Yosemite, strong, bold and resilient standing with power and authority, as if to say, I am somebody. Somebody worthy of their existence, worthy of the magnitude of their capabilities despite the dream haters who resist it. Despite the violent and unforgiving storms of life that may blow their way testing the strength of their backbone, fighting for survival day to day.

I see women rising stepping out on faith letting their voices and courageous actions be known, digging deep within themselves to go places they've never gone. Rising above and beyond the glass ceilings that may plague their dreams, reaching as if they are going to the mountaintops of the Himalayas despite how grand or insurmountable it may seem. I have faith in you and all that you do stand in your power despite the path that you choose. You are women rising!

Rock Your Stage of Life
to Deliver Your Best Performance

It's show time, and guess what? You are the act! Not only are you the act, but you have the potential to dominate your life performance and captivate everyone in your audience. It's an audience that wants to see the best of what you've got. They want to see the real deal. They want to see you! William Shakespeare said it best: "All the world's a stage, and all the men and women merely players; they have their exits and their entrances; and one man in his time plays many parts, his acts being seven ages." The world is waiting for you to rise up and accept the best of what it has to offer you with courage and humility. That's the true meaning of Yes, And to Rock the Stage of Life.

It's giving yourself the freedom to embrace your humanity and live in the here and now by standing in your power and acting on your purpose. It's about coming out from behind the curtains of life and taking center-stage. It's facing the unknown, pursuing your life objectives with intention, and saying, "Yes, And" to those people, places, and things that try to alter your performance to their satisfaction. When you engage in a "Yes, And" mentality, you empower those in your audience or the people around you, because you allow yourself to go with the flow. You allow yourself to demonstrate your flexibility and the willingness to progress in a direction that supports healthy relationships and upward mobility.

This "Yes, And" concept is not new. There's a good chance if you are familiar with the principles of theater, more specifically improvisation, you already understand the meaning of "Yes, And." No worries if you don't. It simply means when your scene partner presents you with a thought or idea you refrain from challenging it by accepting whatever it is that they are offering. You accept it even if it defies logic and conflicts with your values and reasoning.

It is imperative to the scene that improvisers and/or actors avoid judging. It is necessary to be open to new possibilities because if you

> When you engage in a "Yes, And" mentality, you empower those in your audience or the people around you, because you allow yourself to go with the flow. You allow yourself to demonstrate your flexibility and the willingness to progress in a direction that supports healthy relationships and upward mobility.

aren't, the scene stops. There is no momentum to propel the scene forward resulting in a halt to creative expression. As you can see, the sooner you come to the realization of the importance of a having a give and take or Yes, And mindset, the sooner you could benefit from endless opportunities. To know if whether or not you are seeing opportunities, but more importantly seizing opportunities, it's important to ask yourself these relevant questions.

- Are you Yes, And-ing opportunities as they present themselves that could change the course of your life?
- Are you rocking the stage of life or are you letting the stage of life rock you?
- Are you showing up every day, willing to embrace life's challenges to thrive center stage? If not, why?

Mindfulness is Key to Maximizing Your Opportunities

All too often, we minimize our Yes, And opportunities by letting our fears overshadow our potential to make a difference. Therefore, instead of showing up with an open mind to perform, we hide behind the stage of life in regret. Regretting all the things that we could have said or done to elevate our lives and the lives of others. A lack of mindfulness is a key reason why we succumb to our fears simply because we can't see the potential in confirming our opportunities. Our attention is either on the things that have caused us to fear in the past or fearful of things that could potentially happen in the future. As a result, we are not able to respond truthfully. Similar to actors performing on stage, if they are not present mentally they are not able to authentically engage with their scene partner. The gifts that they bring as an actor consequently leave them emotionally disconnected. As a result, they are no longer in a position to respond truthfully.

Actors, just like you, can become victims to the psychological aspects of time which is the origin and manifestation of fear. In *The Power of Now*, Eckhart Tolle says: "Psychological time-which is identification with the past and the continuous compulsive projection into the future…All negativity is caused by an accumulation of psychological time and denial of the present. Unease, anxiety, tension, stress, worry-all forms of fear-are caused by too much future and not enough presence." Therefore, when you are not present and are disengaged from living moment to moment, you surrender your driver's seat and are held captive by your fears. This produces anxiety, self-doubt, and the potential for emotional breakdowns. Unfortunately, many times our regret stems from low self-esteem. As a result, we don't think we are good enough or smart enough to act on impulses that could better our lives. It's for this reason rocking the stage of life looks different for everyone. Why? Because everyone plays a different role at different places and stages in their lives. Within those roles everyone has their own experiences and capabilities, which then impacts their reality and ultimately their courage to accept new challenges. Therefore, don't compare your gifts, talents, skills, and capabilities to others. Don't let them or any unsubstantiated fear cause you to be complacent in evolving into your best self.

You Were Born a Rock Star; Be it, Own it!

You see, I don't know if anyone has told you this lately, but you rock! Let's just be clear that you were inherently born a rock star. You were born to rock the stage of life. You were born with the seeds of resilience, understanding, compassion, imagination, forgiveness, and open-mindedness. This book is not intended to give you something that you already possess. Redundancy has its place and I am pleased to say, it's not here. However, this book was created to reveal and sustain the greatness that lies within you. It was created to allow your individuality to burst through the seams of your fears, repair your tattered spirit, and mend your resilience in a way in which you wear it exceptionally well.

The true nature of your individuality gives you license to take ownership on this so called stage of life. Unfortunately, as we go through life, our innate superpowers to rock the stage of life become impacted not only by our fears but also our focus.

The only difference between you and some of the most formidable improvisers and actors of the world, Meryl Streep, Denzel Washington, and Angela Bassett to name a few, is that their primary objective is to focus on the other actor to respond truthfully under imaginary circumstances. Their focus is what allows them to bring their character to life. As a result, the end product is an actor who is well-deserving of a standing ovation due to her courage and uncompromising presence. The ability to perform honestly under these imaginary circumstances is a credit to her commitment to staying focused. For you, on the other hand, it's not necessary for you to focus on anyone outside of yourself. The only person you need a response from is you. Your focus should be based on your decision to Yes, And by asking yourself key questions. If I Yes, And, to this opportunity will it cause me to grow mentally and spiritually? Will it allow me to express my gifts and talents in a way that enhances my well-being? Does it serve my purpose for existing on this planet? And if so, how?

There are times when you may want to get feedback from others because they are able to see things in you that you may not be able to see in yourself. We are born with blind spots due to our own biases and perception. Being that they are an "outsider" it puts them in a prime position to more readily see your learning gaps, your need to build emotional intelligence or even the strengths you may have.

Sometimes we don't realize how capable we are or how much value we bring until it is brought to our attention. However, the key to accepting feedback so that you can make an informed Yes, And decision, is knowing what to leave on the table and what to run with. For instance, if the feedback is appropriate and on point, it could help you advance in your personal and professional life as well as position you to be your greatest self. On the other hand, if you give too much power to an "outsider" you give less power to the person who matters most—you!

Never give others the power to diminish your performance by dictating how you should show up. In her book, *Grounded*, Nancy M. Dahl says, "When others know more about you than you do, the advantage flips against you-people will use their knowledge of you to make choices for your life. The skill of being a student of you keeps you in the driver's seat of your own bus, which is the only seat you should ever occupy." What seat are you predominately in? When you know where you sit, you will know where you stand when it's time to embrace new opportunities. When it's time to Yes, And, and own the stage of life. Don't let your performance suffer because you are not brave enough to stand in your spotlight. Take center stage, Yes, And to new opportunities, and break a leg.

Time to Rise and Shine!

- ### *Yes, And Rather Than Yes, But*

  It's much easier to conclude your sentences with a Yes, But rather than a Yes, And. A Yes, But keeps weight off of your shoulders. It prevents you from taking on things that have the potential to stretch you so that you can grow into your best self. It keeps you emotionally safe so that you don't have to commit to things that scare you. However, there is a price to pay for your Yes, But. You will never know what you could be or become capable of because you limit your opportunities. You run from things that people who achieve great success tend to face and they become stronger and wiser because of it. On the other hand, a Yes, And has the potential to change your life.

  A Yes, And puts you in the driver's seat because you are willing to go wherever the opportunity takes you providing it is emotionally, physically and mentally safe to do so. It expands your world by exposing you to the world of others, thus facilitating a deeper connection. Furthermore, when you Yes, And you communicate with confidence and power as if to say, "I am willing to step into uncharted territory to see who and what I can become. It is not my fears that will hurt me, but rather my faith that will strengthen me."

  To Yes, And, seek opportunities to identify particular instances when you can substitute a "Yes, But" statement and replace it with a "Yes, And" statement. For instance, if you are at work and are engaged in a conversation that challenges your core values and beliefs, rather than shut down the other persons thoughts and ideas with a "Yes, But" statement, look for ways to affirm their perspective so that the conversation can advance and your relationship can flourish. By taking this approach, it doesn't necessarily mean that you agree with the person or need to feel as though you are compromising your integrity; it just means that you are receptive to engaging in a growth mindset rather than a fixed mindset.

- *Be Willing to Live Beyond Your Comfort Zone*
  Fear of the unknown, if you are not self-aware, will sell you a ticket to the most comfortable place in the world, a place of peace and total relaxation. So much so that people choose to live there for a lifetime. It's also the most expensive and overrated place on earth-your comfort zone. However when you have the power, which you do, you get to choose the size of your comfort zone. How much space you want it to take up in your life is up to you. Strive to make the space as small as possible by Yes, And-ing your fears. When you do, your world will become bigger than you could have possibly ever imagined.

  We as people gravitate to our comfort zone for various reasons. Our comfort zone allows us to feel a sense of security and makes us feel safe from the unknown. It tricks us into sticking to a Yes, But mentality, where we will maintain the status quo and accept things as is. It robs us of our life because it prevents us from trying new things, going to new places, and investing time and energy into meeting new people.

  To transcend beyond your comfort zone see your fears, those things that stop you from saying Yes, And, as an opportunity to grow and change for the better. Let the change represent the chance to connect more deeply with your purpose so you can afford yourself the freedom to live beyond barriers. Let your mental roadblocks—all those things you tell yourself and all those meaningless actions you take that keep you stuck and stagnate your ambitions—inspire you rather than stifle you. Every day, try to do something that scares you. The more you Yes, And and face your fears, the less likely your fears will consume you.

- *Speak Up Your Voice Matters*
Before you can allow yourself to Yes, And, you have to understand that your voice matters. If you don't recognize the value of your voice, Yes, And will become a concept that will be absent from your vocabulary. Your voice is what establishes your place in the world. It's what stops people in their tracks when you say something that resonates in their heart and causes them to take notice of you. When used, it's what brings out the best in you so that you share not only who you are but what you believe in and stand for.

Your voice needs you to advocate for it. To stand up and speak up so that it doesn't remain bottled up inside you only to take up space and never to be heard. It needs you to liberate it so that it is brought to life and expresses your values, creativity, passion and fears. Therefore, when you give power to your voice you not only free yourself to be who you really are, people get to hear the words that make you who you are.

To develop the skills to share your voice it's simply a matter of speaking up. When you have an opportunity to speak up and share your thoughts and ideas, go for it! For instance, if you have an opportunity to provide feedback, do so with the intentions of expanding your comfort zone and boosting your confidence. If you have the chance to use your voice to praise and uplift someone else, be inspired to do so. The more you exercise your voice in various ways, the easier it will be to Yes, And when it matters most.

Conclusion

I BELIEVE IN YOUR RISE!

I believe in your rise! I know that you are capable of achieving great things. I know that you were born to rise as the sun does and shine bright to manifest your boldest dreams. You were born to birth your ideas into existence to create opportunities and make change in the world. A world that is waiting to experience your greatest and most celebrated moments. They will be moments that will inspire you to overcome barriers and transcend beyond your fears.

When you embrace your rise, your fears won't stand a chance of defeating you. They will be reduced to nothing as they lack the sustenance needed to overtake your joy and smother your hopes and dreams. Your fears will pale in comparison to your inner power as you rise to your feet and look to the light.

Let the light shine through you and for you to guide you to a place of understanding. It will show you how to get from where you are to where you want to be if only you believe in you. If only you believe you can rise in the face of adversity by letting go of the things you can't change, but you are intuitive and resilient enough to change the things you can.

As long as you are willing to step out on faith and take the necessary actions based on the 12 principles I've provided in this book, you are well on your way to rising and shining. However, be patient and know that success doesn't happen overnight. Success is cultivated through persistence, tenacity, and work. It is not manufactured from a source outside of yourself. It is derived from within. Therefore, challenge those who get in the way of your rise. Protect it and diminish their power by questioning their motives and setting clear yet reasonable expectations.

As you continue your journey through life, it is my hope that as the storms of life present themselves, you will not fall to your knees but rather you will stand and rise to the occasion to live courageously and unapologetically. You will let the wind at your back strengthen your resilience in the face of adversity so that you have the fortitude to step over molehills, even more so, the ability to climb mountains.

Bottom line, you are destined for greatness. Therefore, bring these principles to life by not just reading and talking about them, but by living them. Let them be at the forefront of your mind when you feel as though your back is against the wall. Let them remove those mental walls so that they are replaced by the metaphorical windows needed to seize opportunities and get perspective of the road that lies ahead. You see, the road that lies ahead of you will take you to great places if you can rise and do the work necessary to put your problems and fears behind you. You have the principles, now it's your time to rise and shine.

SNEAK PEEK

Your body will only go where your mind will take you.
Therefore, if you think great thoughts, you are destined
to go to great places. Just as your gifts and talents are
a terrible thing to waste, so is your mind. Use it wisely.
That is the only insurance that will guarantee safe travels.
Michelle Perdue

First and foremost, I want to thank you for reading this book. A book that strengthened and humbled me in more ways than one. It wasn't always easy to share stories that caused me to feel vulnerable and self-conscious, but I felt the fear and did it anyway. Why? Because you are worth it!

I wanted to create something that was bigger than myself. Something that would be around long after I leave this planet so that I could continue making a difference in your life and the lives of others. However, as I began to get closer to completing this book, I realized I wanted this to be the beginning of many great things to come. So, what did I do? I began writing my second book!

Just as I was excited to write this book and share my life lessons with you, I was also excited about the possibility of creating a book that was made up of powerful messages and life-altering affirmations to inspire and empower you to live your best life.

Similar to this book, my thoughts were to shine light on those areas in your life that may present themselves as barriers to your success as well as the qualities you may want to aspire to, such as resilience, hope, and happiness.

I created this chapter to specifically highlight a few messages and affirmations taken from my next book, titled, *Rise and Shine! Powerful Messages and Affirmations for Living Your Best Life.* It is my hope that you will read them when faced with adversity, but also when life couldn't seem to be better, and you simply want to cuddle up with a good read to be inspired and cultivate a higher level of resilience.

I look forward to staying connected with you! This may be the end of this book, but it doesn't have to be the end of our journey together. I believe there are so many great things in store for you. You just have to be open receiving them and do the work necessary to achieve them. From this point on, let your life performance shine on the stage of life and teach you new lessons. Let it teach you new ways of looking at the world so that you develop the skills of resilience and unapologetically look fear in the face and say, now is my time to rise and shine.

Let the Struggles of Life Propel You, Not Derail You

Embrace the struggles of humanity, for without struggle
your potential awaits abandoned in the depths of your soul,
seeking to be resurrected and birthed into existence.
It's only when you embrace the struggle that you can achieve the
impossible, develop the mental toughness to become unstoppable,
and gain the confidence to rise to the occasion to be phenomenal.
Michelle Perdue

No one ever said that life would be easy and it's a good chance you have learned that to be true. Life will spin you around like a Whirlpool washing machine: tossing you, tumbling you, causing you at times to be dazed and confused. However, if you are not willing to get tossed around and bounce back and live a life of resilience, you will always wonder what could have been possible if you were willing to withstand the turbulence.

Let's face it, it's not easy to take on life's struggles. On its worst days, it can bring you to your knees, crippling you and robbing you of your self-esteem and determination to live a better and more rewarding life. It can make you feel like an unwanted step-child who hungers for attention as she seeks to be heard and hugged in moments of distress. Life can make you want to give up and give in to your fears. It can cause you to relinquish control over your life so that you cease to fight for your integrity, dignity, and humanity.

How about your best days? When you are willing to take on life's struggles in the midst of your best days, this is when your life begins to take on a whole new meaning. For instance, when "life happens" it doesn't stand a chance to weaken your knees, but rather it strengthens your mind and restores courage in your heart. It's your courage that allows you to surrender your fears and welcome the struggles life brings. It empowers you to fail forward and learn from your mistakes so that you can ask better questions in response to your failures. It allows you to challenge yourself to look deeper and discover the root of your fears.

So, let your struggles change you not chain you. When you allow them to change you, you allow them to create new directions and opportunities in your life. You allow them to open your eyes with curiosity and develop a hunger to live a life of passion. When you allow them to chain you, you allow them to restrict you by creating barriers to your ambitions. These barriers seek not to cleanse your mind, heart, and soul so that you are prepared for the uncertainties of life, but rather distort your vision of how strong and powerful you really are. Therefore, go ahead and let the world spin you around like a Whirlpool clothes dryer. Let it dry your tears and fluff your feathers so that you can soar amongst the birds in the skies to become your potential.

I am not afraid to rise up in the face of my struggles.

Live Big: You Were Born to Be a Giant

You were born a giant, so live according to your size.
Take up space in this world as if you own it and have a right to occupy it.
Spread your wings as if you were a butterfly roaming the sky full of
color and wonder. Stand firm on your feet and let your legs
walk with purpose. Let them lead you down roads less traveled
for self-discovery and character building opportunities.
Let your posture be as erect as the rising sun causing your chest
to bulge with pride and an overwhelming sense of purpose.
Michelle Perdue

Are you playing small in the world? Are you letting your blessing erode and decay like rotten tomatoes that have dropped to the soil that gave it life? Have your ambitions shriveled up like a prune left in the desert with no salvation in sight? If so, I want to reconnect your mind. Your mind has fooled you and led you astray. Made you believe that your intellect, complexion, or abilities were inferior to others. There is nothing inferior about you.

I want to plant seeds of resilience in your thoughts so that you realize the magnitude of your potential. A potential so big, even the giant sequoias of Yosemite would pale in comparison to what you can offer the world. It is my hope that these seeds of resilience will strengthen your power to stand firm when adversity comes knocking at your door, requiring you to face your fears. And when that times comes, rather than become meek, you will rise to become your biggest and boldest self.

When you play small, I believe the rainbows of the world are robbed of their vibrant and illustrious colors. The sun becomes diminished in light. People around you show up only as a fraction of themselves. Why? Because they lack the light to shine to their full potential. You see, when you play big, your light becomes infectious. It's your light that is generated from playing big that will nurture their souls and enrich their lives. They become alive. They become energized, no longer complacent in achieving their own aspirations.

If you can imagine how you're playing big can affect others, imagine how it can affect you. When you play big, you are unfazed by rejection or the ideal of perfection. You give yourself permission to create your own reality by validating your truths and honoring your values. You embrace your vision until it is manifested and has come to fruition. When you play big, you seize moments of opportunity that will elevate your life and broaden your horizons. So you see, playing big grants you things that would otherwise be impossible to achieve if you weren't willing to take up space in this world and be the giant that you are. Live full and live big.

I am growing into myself so that I can live bold and live big.

Be Silent to Appreciate the Voice from Within

Be still. Your true gifts can only be received in your moments of silence.
For when you are still with body and mind,
the whispers of the universe are heard loud and clear.
Therefore, don't be fooled by the distractions of mankind
and the worldly noise around you;
let the whispers of the divine dance in your ears,
awaken your spirit, and enrich your soul.
Michelle Perdue

Slow down and become one with your thoughts. Let your thoughts teach you and guide to a place of self-discovery so that you learn more about yourself and the world than anyone could possibly teach you. It's when you slow down, the ambiguity of your thoughts becomes clear and the burden that lies within your heart becomes resolved and results in a place of understanding.

Learn to embrace your thoughts; it's in the whispers of their voices that they are screaming to be heard, to be deliberately acted upon, and desperate to be recognized for validation and acceptance. So be generous and give your thoughts a voice. Don't let the noise of the world smother their contributions to your humanity. Let it breathe by giving it life in pursuit of your joy and happiness so that you empower your mind, which then empowers your thoughts and ultimately your actions.

When you make time to engage with your thoughts, it's a gift that you not only give to yourself, but a gift that you are able to use in conjunction with your purpose to be a gift to someone else. Why? Because your thoughts aim you in the direction of your calling, that thing that you were born to do. Therefore, when you listen intently you gain the knowledge and insight to learn how best to empower others. When you empower others in an authentic and meaningful way, you set the tone for a life of abundance and prosperity for everyone involved.

Are you ready to live a life beyond your comfort zone by listening to your heart and becoming one with your mind? Are you ready to slow down and find the meaning in your mess by not letting fear force-feed you thoughts that are destructive and damaging to your growth? If so, starting today, starting right now, take inventory of your thoughts to become aware of their daily impact on your life.

Challenge the validity of your thoughts. Challenge the role they want to serve in your life and if the role tries to overshadow your character and take center stage, you must rise to the occasion and claim your place as the star of your show. Remember, you are not an extra in life. You were born to be the star of your show. So, learn to own and embrace your thoughts. When you do, you not only own the stage, but you are equipped to conquer the world!

I am mindful of my thoughts and how they impact my life.

REFERENCES

Agnes, Michael & Sparks, N. Andrew (2002) *Webster's New World Compact School AND Office Dictionary* (Fourth Edition), Canada: Wiley Publishing.

Brown, B. (2010). *The Gifts of Imperfection*. Minnesota: Hazelden.

Dispenza, Joe. (2012) *Breaking the Habit of Being Yourself*. Australia: Hay House.

Hanson, R. (2018). *Resilient*. New York: Harmony Books.

Harvey, S. (2016). *Jump*. New York: Harper Collins

Henry, T. (2015). *Louder Than Words*. New York: Portfolio/Penguin.

Johnson, Amber, "Examining associations between racism, internalized shame, and self-esteem among African Americans," *Cogent Psychology* April 7, 2020

Examining associations between racism, internalized shame, and self-esteem ...: EBSCOhost (hclib.org)

Leonard, K. & Yorton T. (2015). *Yes, And*. New York: Harper Collins

Reivich, K. & Shatte, A. (2002). *The Resilience Factor*. New York: Three Rivers Press

Robbins, M. (2009). *be yourself*. California: Jossey-Bass.

Schwartz, A. (2020). *The Post Traumatic Growth Guidebook*. Wisconsin: PESI.

Tolle, E. (2004). *The Power of Now*. Canada: Namaste

Ungar, M. (2018). *Change Your World*. Ontario: Southerland House

Websites Consulted

https://www.mayoclinichealthsystems.org

https://www.health.harvard.edu

https://www.quotes-positive.com

https://www.brainyquote.com

https://www.bbc.co.uk

https://www.habitsforwellbeing.com

https://self-compassion.org

https://www.researchgate.net

https://www.inspiringquotes.us

https://www.psychologytoday.com

https://dreamachieversacademy.com

How to Develop Self-Compassion | Psychology Today

ABOUT THE AUTHOR

MICHELLE PERDUE, M.Ed., is a motivational and highly impactful Keynote Speaker, author and coach. She authoritatively speaks on the topic of resilience and is best known for her rare ability to deliver performance-based presentations to transform and engage her audience.

Michelle has presented at various companies including Land O' Lakes, Johnson & Johnson, and Ecolab. She has also presented at the Minnesota Women's Lawyers Conference, TeamWomen Conference and the Domestic Abuse Project Annual Fundraiser event, among other notable organizations.

As a graduate of the University of Minnesota, the Ruskin School of Acting and a veteran of the Army Reserves, Michelle has continuously proven that with hard work and the motivation to succeed, life is full of endless possibilities.

Michelle facilitates impactful workshops and delivers engaging keynote presentations to elevate the lives of others with transformational tools and resources. In addition, Michelle has written and produced two poetry CD's titled, *Journey: Poetry of Hurt Healing* and *Hope* and *Resilient I Am: Inspirational Poems for Healing and Thriving With and Beyond Cancer.*

To learn more about Michelle and/or to book Michelle as your next Keynote Speaker, workshop facilitator or coach, feel free to visit www.MichellePerdueSpeaks.com. This includes *Rise and Shine! A Journal for Becoming the Powerful and Resilient You*, which compliments this book wonderfully.

ACKNOWLEDGEMENTS

I am beyond grateful to those of you who helped make this book possible. For those of you who took the time to read my book and offer invaluable feedback, I want you to know that you are truly appreciated. Therefore, I would like to thank Courtney Watson, Jody Levy, Kristi Romo, Jill Nokleby, Sandy Checel, Christina Checel, and Troy Perdue for your time and support in helping to make this book possible. Your feedback and attention to detail gave me the guidance needed to work harder and make better choices.

I would also like to thank those who read my manuscript and offered to write testimonials. Nancy M. Dahl, Julie Burton, Teresa Thomas, Dr. Jermaine Davis and Barbara Butts-Williams—your kind words and generous spirits mean a lot to me. I am proud to say that each of you made my heart smile and I want you to know that I thank you and appreciate you.

I would also like to express my appreciation and gratitude to Pam Borton for her support in writing the Foreword to this book. Your insight and words of wisdom are appreciated and truly inspiring. Whether you realize it or not, you inspire me to rise to my potential. Your leadership abilities and commitment to the uplifting of women is nothing less than extraordinary. You are a force in this world and I thank you for being you.

I would like to thank those of you who encouraged me to keep going. It was your encouragement that inspired me to work harder and fight to the end to complete this book and for that I am truly grateful. This includes my wonderful family and close friends as well as my accountability partner. Duane Martinz, you are the best accountability partner a gal could ask for. I am so lucky to have been partnered with you. It is my hope that your book, *Becoming Your Own Champion,* will touch many lives as you have mine. Without all of you, I would be telling a different story. You encouraged and elevated me to rise in my darkest moments only to emerge and embrace the light from within. Thank you for who you are and all that you do.

I would also like to thank my awesome photographer, Dani Werner, at Dani Werner Photography. Dani, your work consistently speaks for it self-captivating, rich and priceless. Also, I would like to thank my make-up artist, Amber Young, and hair stylist Gina Jones, for helping me to look my best. Your skillful and creative abilities helped to instill the confidence needed for me to show up as my best self. Finally, thank you all for your kind and generous contributions. It was because of you and the others that I was able to rise and shine and turn my vision into a reality.

With love and gratitude,

Michelle Perdue

Made in the USA
Monee, IL
16 July 2021